(Continued from front flap)

now taking place. *Part Five* is a summary and concluding statement.

Dr. Wyckoff has dealt with the important question of Christian education simply and clearly, without sacrificing the depth of his message or the thoroughness of its approach. His book should prove an excellent and immediately helpful guide for Christian educators in getting fully acquainted with their task and in carrying it on. It will also be valuable to college and seminary students in introducing them to the field of Christian education and in helping them to organize and summarize their own points of view.

THE AUTHOR

D. Campbell Wyckoff studied at Columbia University and received the degrees of B.S., A.M., and Ph.D. from New York University, majoring in religious education. He taught in national missions schools in North Carolina and Tennessee, and was staff assistant and Assistant Secretary, units of Rural Church and Indian Work, with the Presbyterian Board of National Missions from 1942 to 1947. He taught in the Department of Religious Education, School of Education, at New York University from 1947 to 1954, becoming chairman of the department in 1950. In the fall of 1954, Dr. Wyckoff became Thomas W. Synnott Professor of Christian Education at the Princeton Theological Seminary, Princeton, New Jersey.

The TASK *of*
CHRISTIAN
EDUCATION

The TASK of CHRISTIAN EDUCATION

by

D. Campbell Wyckoff

Philadelphia
THE WESTMINSTER PRESS

PRINTED IN THE UNITED STATES OF AMERICA

CONTENTS

Part Three

THE TRANSFORMATION OF PERSONALITY

PREFACE

THIS BOOK is written with two purposes in mind. The first is to try to clear up some of the confusion that exists today in Christian education theory and practice. The second is to provide a guide for Christian educators in getting acquainted with their task and carrying it on.

The book is intended for church school teachers, for superintendents, for directors of Christian education, for ministers, for members of boards and committees of Christian education, and for others who are deeply concerned with the problem.

The contents have developed in a somewhat unusual way. As the outline was being developed it became clear that a great deal of the material in the book should be written directly to the workers who are closest to the practice of Christian education. Full outlines of the proposed contents of each chapter were prepared, and as opportunity presented itself they were worked out in detail as lectures and talks before various groups and classes. In most cases they were recorded on tape, sometimes two or more versions of the same material. After transcription they were edited and completely rewritten. Even the original outline of chapters was changed in the process in order to try to state the essential message briefly and clearly. Nowhere have the plans or content of the book been sacrificed, however, to the demands of the lecture platform or the classroom.

My gratitude is very great to those who gave me the opportunity to speak parts of the pages to them:

The East Orange (N.J.) Council of Churches, at its annual meeting and its leadership training school.

The Niagara Falls (N.Y.) Council of Religious Education, at one
of its public meetings.

The Immanuel Union Church, Staten Island, N.Y., at a meeting
of the parents of the older boys and girls in its church school.

The Parents' Association of the Reformed Church of Bronxville,
N.Y.

The Westminster Presbyterian Church, Buffalo, N.Y., at the opening parents' meeting of the church year. (This session was not
recorded.)

The Protestant Council of New York City, at its observance of
Christian Education Day. (This session was not recorded.)

The summer institute for Lutheran pastors, held at Wagner College, Staten Island, N.Y.

St. Mark's Methodist Church, Brooklyn, N.Y., at a meeting of the
teachers and officers of its church school.

My class in the philosophy of religious education, in the School of
Education of New York University.

Special thanks are due to Mrs. Mabel Barton Brown, of New
York City, and to my aunt, Miss A. Amelia Wyckoff, whose
prompt and accurate transcriptions of the tape recordings made
the writing possible. My aunt also checked the entire manuscript,
making numerous suggestions as to style.

The reader will benefit most from the book if he keeps its plan
in mind. Part One serves as an introduction, and deals with the
current status of Christian education in theory (Chapter I), aims
(Chapter II), and practice (Chapter III). Part Two deals one by
one with the most pertinent aspects of the Christian life: the
need for a way of life that is definitely Christian (Chapter IV),
Christian doctrine (Chapter V), the Bible (Chapter VI), the
Church (Chapter VII), growth in ability to believe (Chapter
VIII), and the reality of Jesus Christ as him in whom we live
and move and have our being (Chapter IX). Part Three under-
takes to interpret the meaning of personality and the ways in
which personality may become Christian (Chapters X, XI, XII),
leading to a summary statement (Chapter XIII) of a fundamen-

tal theory of Christian education. Part Four deals with some of the more important specifics: curriculum (Chapter XIV), methods (Chapter XV), the responsibilities of the individual, the home, the church, the school, and the community (Chapter XVI), and some of the promising developments now taking place (Chapter XVII). Part Five is a final summary and concluding statement.

A great deal of ground is covered in the pages that follow. There are many important subjects that are only mentioned or dealt with so briefly as to be unsatisfactorily handled. Some important matters have been omitted. I have had to keep my purpose strictly in mind: to give a picture of the whole task of Christian education that will be stimulating and broadening to the worker in the field. If I am able to extend his vision, stretch his imagination, and encourage him to try out some promising possibilities, the aim will have been accomplished.

D. CAMPBELL WYCKOFF.

Part One

THE STATUS OF CHRISTIAN EDUCATION

Chapter 1

EMERGING FROM CONFUSION

THE LEADERS of Christian education are less confused today than they have been for some years. They are just emerging from a period of critical restudy to determine the theoretical bases upon which they may develop sound practice.

What the leaders think gives guidance to the Church in what it does about Christian education, but does not guarantee that it will be reflected in the practice of the local church. It is a mistake to assume that the prevailing thought of a period will find its way into all or even most of the programs of individual churches and church schools.

In order that the present status of thought on Christian education may be understood, it is important to review the history of the best of the thought and practice of its exponents during the last three decades.

A PERIOD OF CREATIVE DEVELOPMENT

Not many years ago Christian education seemed very sure of its direction. Along with other types of education it had discovered new methods and new ways of affecting personality. Christian educators were convinced that these could be used to transform and to reconstruct the experience of children, youth, and adults into the ways of the Christian life.

It was guided by sound psychological principles, and with their use it sought to develop the mature and integrated Christian individual. It was motivated by deep social concern, and attempted to build the kind of personality that would be effective in dealing with the problems of the community, the nation, and the world on the basis of Christian standards.

This period reached its climax in the 1920's. During that decade, building on work previously done, various denominational curriculums of Christian education were revised and new denominational curriculums instituted. Interdenominational and university groups prepared new materials, making them more child-centered, more interesting to the pupil, and more directly related to his own life experiences. It was felt that if they could be prepared with the pupil himself in mind, becoming less subject-matter-centered and more life-centered, they would be more effective instruments in helping to produce the Christian life.

Methods of teaching were greatly changed. Learning by rote, memory, and drill gave way to the use of activities and projects. This necessitated new kinds of equipment, changes in the schedule of the church school, and new approaches to leadership education.

Churches needed more space, and space better adapted to this new kind of program. Large projects in church building were undertaken in which the emphasis was not only upon beautiful and fitting sanctuaries, but also upon providing church schools, church houses, and parish buildings that would care for the needs of Christian education on a seven-days-a-week basis.

It was during this period that the attempt to take care realistically of the total responsibility of Christian education led to the widespread acceptance and growth of such agencies as the weekday church school, the vacation church school, and the leadership training school. These were attempts to improve and dignify a task that was being taken more seriously than ever before.

CURTAILMENT AND CRITICISM

In the early 1930's the great depression made it impossible to continue the program of Christian education on the scale that had been developed in the previous decade. Money was not available to continue large building operations. Retrenchments were necessary in professional personnel in the local church and in personnel available for curriculum planning, construction, and supervision.

At the same time, spurred on by a new interest in theological study, many leaders in the field began to wonder if perhaps some of the failures to achieve the high purposes that they had set for themselves might not be due to a sacrificing of the essential message of the Christian faith to the new methods and procedures they had been using. Nagging misgivings plagued Christian education from that time on, misgivings about its very foundations and the place of its methods within the total process of bringing personality to levels of achievement that might conscientiously be called Christian. These misgivings were keenly felt at the local church level, at the denominational level, and at the level of interdenominational planning.

When the nation became involved in World War II, any optimistic views about the nature of man that might have been held previously were soon dispelled by the realistic tragedy of war and the spectacle of totalitarianism.

Faith in education itself declined. It was felt that perhaps too much reliance had been placed upon education as a solution for the world's ills. Public education throughout the nation had been almost completely achieved. Illiteracy had been greatly reduced, accompanied by an unprecedented increase in the amount of reading material, including newspapers and magazines of public opinion, available to the general public. Yet international problems had not been solved, but aggravated.

A more pessimistic view of the nature of man and of education echoed the doctrines that a growing company of theologians had been trying to impress upon the American mind for over a decade.

The individual teacher and the local church do not always respond rapidly to change and suggestions of change. There had been a great deal of resistance to the changes in methods and procedures that had come during the 1920's. There were many churches that had not adopted them; such churches felt definitely at sea in trying to use the curriculums then being introduced.

The change in approach that came with the critical period resulted in even greater confusion as those churches which regarded themselves as up-to-date in Christian education discovered that they were being severely criticized by advocates of even newer ideas of what Christian education theory and practice should be.

Very little experimentation had been done in trying to bring together a sound methodology, based upon psychological and social principles, and the traditional message of the Christian faith, which was being more and more re-emphasized.

RESTUDY

In the middle of the decade of the 1940's it became imperative for many of the denominations and Christian education leaders to rethink their position almost entirely, to develop new curriculums, to make new suggestions of methods, and to develop suggestions for organization and administration of the local church that would bring the churches into line with the new theological trends.

The International Council of Religious Education was given responsibility for gathering together an inclusive group of Christian education leaders from the entire country to try to come to some agreements as to the bases for Christian education. Their report was published by the International Council of Religious Education in mimeographed form in 1946–1947 and was digested by Paul H. Vieth and published under his authorship as *The Church and Christian Education* by Bethany Press, 1947. This famous study of Christian education resulted in something of a meeting of minds. This in turn resulted in new direction for the process of Christian education and helped particularly at the denominational level to direct planning in the field.

The denominations, as a rule, took the responsibilities necessary for the revisions to be made in curriculum and in administration and organization. Co-operative planning of general policy and strategy was done through the International Council of Religious Education, and is now being done through its successor, the Division of Christian Education of the National Council of the Churches of Christ in the U.S.A.

We are now at the place in the life of the local church when in some cases the revised curriculums are being used, after experimental periods of several years. In other cases the revised curriculums have only begun to come into use in the local church. In still others they have been so delayed that they have not yet reached the local church level.

A New Opportunity

Now that the international situation, serious as it is, does not demand our undivided attention, now that increased funds are available for improved programs, and now that the theory of Christian education shows promise of becoming to some extent stabilized, we see the possibility in the years that are immediately ahead of a new period of creative thought, action, and achievement akin in promise to the period of the 1920's.

We cannot know what the future holds, but we hope that in the coming years we may, with something of a merging of the achievements of the 1920's and the theological studies and rediscoveries of the later period, come to the place where we can establish a process of Christian education that has real validity and integrity for our day. Thus the confusion that besets us even now may be to some extent allayed.

Chapter 2

WHAT CHRISTIAN EDUCATION
SETS OUT TO DO

To REDUCE the confusion in Christian education it is essential that we rethink our purposes in line with sound educational procedures and a sound theology.

Religious education is the guided process of helping growing persons to achieve at each stage of their growth such habits, skills, attitudes, appreciations, knowledges, ideas, ideals, and intentions as will enable them at each stage to achieve an ever more integrated personality, competent and satisfying living in their social environment, and increasing co-operativeness with God and man in the reconstruction of society into a fellowship of persons. This is the definition of religious education that the late Samuel L. Hamilton worked out during his years in the leadership of the Department of Religious Education in New York University's School of Education. It defines religious education as a process that does not exclude other faiths. Carried on within a Christian interpretation of the nature of God and his will, and an understanding and practice of the reality of Christ in the life of man, it may become adapted to Christian education.

MARKS OF THE CHRISTIAN LIFE

The definition speaks of habits, skills, attitudes, appreciations, knowledges, ideas, ideals, and intentions. These are qualities of personality, but as here stated they are not specific enough because they lack Christian content. In order to make them standard for Christian education we must be definite about the specific attributes that are characteristic of Christian living. Of course, the specific forms they will take will be somewhat different for children, youth, and adults, because the experiences and achievements of human life are different at different age levels. Nevertheless we may generalize to some extent upon the specific forms that they will take.

The Christian life will be one of devotion to the enhancement of personal and social living, particularly through knowledge of and adherence to the will and purpose of God for individual life and for the life of society.

Christian character and personality will be distinguished by the achievement of an understanding of the world, its resources and its needs. This means the natural world and the ways in which we may co-operate with it to achieve a fuller and richer life. It also means the social world; unless we understand the persons around us, and the very core of their integrity, we cannot help to meet their needs in any real sense.

Christian personality will be marked by an understanding of God's purposes, will, and plan, and of their working out in the world. Christian education has too often seemed concerned merely about the social relationships that exist between man and man. But it is not truly Christian until it thinks of these relations, central as they are, in terms of the dimension that transcends them. God is sovereign; unless his sovereignty is recognized by men in their working together in the world, his will may not be done and the goals of Christian personality and a Christian society may not be achieved.

The Christian person understands his own nature. This includes an understanding of his abilities, the ways they may be used in the world to meet its needs, and the ways he may use them to meet his own needs. Self-knowledge and self-understanding are basic to the effective work of any individual within society. What gives him joy? What gives him satisfaction? What are the distinguishing marks of his way of life? These, as well as the negative factors in his personality, are what he must know about himself. Of late years a great deal of work has been done to help individuals to know themselves in order that they may be more effective in the world around them.

Christian persons are personally and socially absorbed in the processes of living through which Christian truth, Christian values, and Christian understandings are to be gained, and through which they may be put into practice. It is important to be specific here and to list some of the more important of these processes.

They *think* carefully and analytically; they are not satisfied with unsupported emotion and feeling. They are true, objectively and subjectively, in their judgments and in their relationships.

They know *friendship,* the deep and abiding bond between persons that means understanding and leads to effectiveness.

Their lives are lives of *love.* Love is the central emotion and dominant motive of the Christian life. It is ethical love, involving self-giving and the understanding of other persons. It is not sentimental, wrapped up in itself and given to enjoying itself. Rather it seeks the welfare of the loved one, and seeks to love, to feel, and to be deeply concerned far beyond the boundaries that usually circumscribe the life of the individual.

They *teach,* reaching out to other persons with the truth, and trying to guide the experience of others into truth.

They express themselves through *the arts.* In music, painting, and the other arts human life attempts to express itself, to express the truth, and to say realistically and beautifully what it is that gives life its heart and meaning.

They *play,* and in doing so not only release themselves but come closer than in any other activity to those with whom they have had little or no contact before. Play leads us to relax the inhibitions that have kept us away from other persons, and is thus a condition for fellowship.

They *worship,* and thus draw near, singly, and corporately, to the heart of God, bringing their achievements, failures, difficulties, frustrations, joys, and disappointments to be looked at, meditated upon, and evaluated in terms of his will and purpose. In worship we find together what his will and purpose are. In it we achieve new joys and reach new heights of devotion that re-create and renew us. In it there is created the possibility of our becoming more effective Christians. Worship is the climactic experience of the Christian life. It is both deeply individual and profoundly social in its implications. It is in worship that man, nature, and God come most closely together and men find their most meaningful relationships.

They engage in *social reconstruction*. This is the area in which we experiment with insights into God's will and purpose. In remedial social activities we find many of the experiences that lead us to know what the truth is. We try out newly discovered ideas to see whether or not they really have validity for the Christian life. Our social life is an experiment in Christian living; it is a proving ground for our Christian faith. Faith that has not been taken out into social life and tried out remains unproved, hypothetical, and theoretical.

This is one of the reasons why *the missionary enterprise* is so important for Christian life and the Christian Church. It is one of the reasons why *evangelism* is so important for the life of the church and the Christian community. In missions and evangelism perhaps pre-eminently, we test out those ideals that are most profoundly Christian. But missions and evangelism include the basic ingredient of social action or social service, in a spirit of sharing and self-giving fellowship.

Undergirding all these processes is the process of *study:* careful, analytical, guided study which penetrates to the core of problems and is not satisfied with any merely superficial solutions on the basis of limited data easily at hand. Study is the activity by which we probe deeply and in which we use reason, the most characteristic resource that human life has. In study we use reason, tempered by profound feeling and tested subjective experience, in order to gain satisfactory new direction. Study that is not informed by Christian faith and the truth of Christ fails of its highest potential.

Study implies *intelligent belief*. Intelligent belief in turn implies knowledge, the ability to interpret that knowledge for oneself and others, and the development in personal and group living of the quality of *faith*. Intelligent belief involves knowledge of the Bible, understanding of it as revealed truth, and ability to interpret it. It involves knowledge of Christian truth and ability to interpret it: the reality and will of God, the condition of man and his possibilities, the person and work of Christ, how man is redeemed, what the Church is for and how it functions, and human destiny. It involves knowledge of the history of religion, and especially of the Christian religion, and ability to see our own vital role and that of our time in the achievement of the Church's universal and eternal purpose. It involves ability to see and interpret the relationships between religion and other phases of one's life, between religious knowledge and other types of knowledge.

This implies the development of a philosophy of life. For the Christian it will be a Christian philosophy of life for it will be informed by Christian knowledge and will be interpreted in terms of the Christian faith. The crux of Christian philosophy is the experience that the individual has of the reality and truth of God in Christ, the Christ revealed in the Bible and revealed as the living Christ in the minds and hearts of men throughout the ages and even down to our own time.

When the living Christ is known and experienced, belief becomes more than intellectual assent. It takes on the quality of a living and vital faith. We say that the aim of education is that man shall know the truth and become free through allegiance to it. We interpret this in terms of Christian education and say that its aim is that man shall know Christ, who is the truth of God in human life, and that man shall become free through wholehearted and complete allegiance to him.

All these are processes in which the Christian person is deeply absorbed. His own personal life is taken up with them, as are his family life, his community life, his relationships with his neighbors, his relationships within his church, and his relationships in the larger areas of society. When we say that he is absorbed in this kind of process, we mean that he gives himself to the living in thoroughgoing fashion of those processes through which an understanding of God, an understanding of the universe around him, an understanding of other persons, and self-understanding may grow. All these qualities are ends that we are trying to achieve through Christian education and through the total life of the Christian community in the church and elsewhere.

THE AIMS OF CHRISTIAN EDUCATION

The aim of Christian education is to nurture the Christian life. The marks of the Christian life just surveyed clearly imply that such nurture involves Christian instruction, the redemption of the individual, and the redemption of society.

Christian education cannot achieve its purposes unless it instructs the pupil in the basic aspects of the Christian faith and the Christian life. We do not intend to raise a generation of religious illiterates. While it is possible to become a good person and to lead a worth-while adult life without having received direct instruction in Christian truth and Christian values, Christian education itself cannot be carried on with integrity if it neglects Christian instruction.

We are deeply concerned that direct Christian instruction in faith and doctrine shall take place; that our pupils may know, live with, and learn to love the Bible; and that they may gain from the Bible and from the history of the Church the fundamental doctrines and teachings that have always led and motivated Christians. In our day these doctrines and teachings will be rethought, not to change their fundamental nature, for no such change is necessary, but rather in order that they may speak distinctly to the needs of our day.

But we cannot be satisfied with instruction alone, to leave Christian education at the intellectual level. The second aim of Christian education voices our concern that the Christian life may be lived and that Christian character may be built. This includes three concerns: that Christian education may be effective in helping persons to develop lives of integrity; that it may be effective in helping persons to develop lives that are socially aware; and that it may be effective in helping persons to live in full awareness of God.

Christian education seeks to develop the qualities of Christian living within the pupil's experience, those qualities that characterize Christian personality at its best and most effective. In the practice of Christian education they are understood to be graded in accordance with the various levels of pupil experience and achievement.

In spite of the fact that we stress direct Christian instruction and the importance of the qualities of personal Christian living, we cannot say that we have achieved the objectives of Christian education until we have so changed society that the very processes of our community living help persons to become Christian rather than stand in the way of their becoming Christian. Christian education must espouse as one of its important and necessary aims the rebuilding of the community so that it will help rather than hinder the process of religious and Christian growth.

These aims, of course, are to be shared by all the persons and groups interested in the process of the Christian education of the individual. Since the church has a recognized and essential part in that process, some indication should be given of the interpretation of these aims in terms of the church's distinctive task in Christian nurture. A church may well state its Christian education aims in terms of such outcomes as these in the lives of its pupils: intelligent belief, Christian commitment, Christian character, churchmanship, and participation in the redemption of the community.

With aims like these it should be possible for us to move forward into the next period in Christian education constructively and creatively. We should be able to move ahead confident that we are true to the Christian faith, that we are sound in our emphasis on Christian living and Christian character, and that we are not neglecting the social aspects of our task.

Chapter 3

CHRISTIAN EDUCATION IN ACTION: AN OVERVIEW

THE AIMS of Christian education cannot be automatically achieved. It is only wishful thinking that would indicate that children, youth, and adults become Christian without careful planning of the Christian education program. Part of our stewardship is to plan with care.

This chapter will survey as a whole the procedures that should be, and to a great extent are now, in common use in Christian education. When we have looked at them as a whole, we may be able to get some idea of the strengths and weaknesses of our policies and program.

Many churches are not using anything like a carefully worked out program of Christian education. Nevertheless, many of the elements to be discussed here will be found in most programs, at least in some rudimentary form. Leaders might well check what they are doing in their own local churches against some such outline as this in order to get an idea of points at which their programs need improvement or expansion.

DETERMINING SPECIFIC OBJECTIVES

Any program should be founded upon inclusive and representative general objectives. But the general objectives of Christian education need translation into specific form in every situation. The principle of grading, for one thing, should be applied to them in order to understand specifically what they mean for the child, the youth, and the adult at his own level of experience and achievement. This requires an analysis of the nature and needs of the pupil, a close knowledge of the individual and the group. For many leaders the responsibility will be for more than one age group, so that this will involve a working knowledge of a variety of groups encompassing all age levels and a variety of individuals encompassing various levels of achievement.

Part of our equipment will be a fairly comprehensive knowledge of what may be learned from the psychology of human development. What is to be expected from the child at each level of development? What is the significance of adolescence, and when are its distinctive needs met? What are the characteristics of maturity, the life of the Christian adult? What are the characteristics of old age; how may old age be redeemed so that it too may be Christian?

The psychology of human development can help us at point after point in our understanding of the Christian life and the way in which it develops. Our understanding of the Christian life will begin with the general processes of life and growth, for we realize that it is human life as it is actually lived and experienced that is redeemed, transformed, and reconstructed as God in Christ takes hold of the individual, the group, and society.

Sociology also can help us, for we know that the environment, the society in which the individual lives, the way it is organized, and the kind of resources that it places at his disposal will have a telling effect upon him and upon the kind of life that he leads. The social analysis of the community, the family, and the group within which the individual lives is very important in helping us to understand him, his motivations, and his behavior.

Educators sometimes fail to pay enough attention to the philosophical and theological understandings that relate to the nature and needs of the pupil. It is probably asking too much even to suggest that the average church school teacher become an expert philosopher or a proficient theologian. Nevertheless it is rather important that some basic understanding of the nature of man, the nature of the child, the way in which growth takes place, the significance of growth, and the kind of outcomes that are expected in terms of personal growth and achievement be reached by every responsible church school teacher and leader. This means that time should be given to a consideration of the fundamentals of the faith, Christian truth and doctrine, in order that the relationships between God, the universe, society, and the individual may be understood, and in order that the individual himself may come to a deep self-understanding.

All this may seem rather remote from the individual child, youth, or adult. But on the basis of the psychological needs and nature of the individual, his place in society understood in terms of a sociological analysis of the environment in which he lives and his relationships to it, and a philosophical and theological understanding of his place in the universe and his relations to the other elements of creation, we come to the place where it is possible to see him as an individual in his setting and thus to analyze his particular nature and his particular needs.

What do we look for when we actually come to the analysis of the life of the individual? We look at his home life, to see what his relationships are there: his place in the home, his achievements there, and possibly his frustrations. We look at his school life, for here we get some clue to his intellectual development and his relationships with those who are his leaders as well as with those who are of his own age and level of development, thought, understanding, and feeling. We look at his recreational life in order to be able to see what he does with his leisure time; his leisure time is likely to be as much a clue to his nature and his needs as any one other aspect, for here as a rule he has an unparalleled chance to choose for himself what he will do, giving an indication of the kind of needs that he himself feels, consciously or unconsciously.

We look at other aspects of his intellectual life besides those within the school. Some clue to this will of course be found in the school, but as a rule his intellectual life will show up best as we talk with him informally about the things that he is thinking about, the questions and problems that he is raising, the kind of conclusions and generalizations that he is coming to about the serious affairs of the world and society, and his own philosophy of life. It is interesting of course that in a very concrete and specific way even the little child is working out his philosophy of life. It will become more abstract, more profound and far-reaching, as he becomes older and more experienced.

In all these relationships of the home, school, play group, and the like, we are particularly concerned with the things that he is interested in, the things that he spends his time on, and the kind of identification that he makes with other things in his environment. Interest and attention are clues to motivation. The things that we are interested in, the things we will attend to, are likely to indicate the deep creative springs of our personalities. Thus the things the child, youth, or adult takes an interest in will become, in a sense, projective clues as to what is going on within his own personality and what his character structure may be.

We are interested also in talking with him and in watching him as he lives and works with his fellow men to discover what his conception of his own role in life is. Every individual has a picture of himself. He sees himself in his relationships to other persons. That conception of his role, or his place in life, is a direct clue as to the kind of personality and character he has developed; and it is a clue to his level of achievement. That conception of his role will show up in his relationships to other individuals, in his relations to groups, in his relations to his family, and in his relations to the community.

Out of all of this we construct a personality study of the individual. We shall thus be able to arrive at some idea of his personality configuration. This means that we shall have come as close as possible to an understanding of him as he really is.

Contrast this with the usual superficial kind of judgment that we make about persons and individuals with whom we come into contact. Too many teachers and administrators are given to snap judgments about the persons they deal with. They do not go to the trouble of finding out who these people really are. They do not bother to watch them in many of their relationships. They see them perhaps in one relationship; they may be struck favorably or unfavorably, and this superficial judgment becomes the basis of their working with the individual from that time on.

We must reflect on the fact that these configurations and understandings of the individual must change from time to time. In Christian education we are interested in re-creating personality, reconstructing personality, and transforming personality. Yet time and again we find teachers and administrators who are unconsciously unwilling to grant that re-creation, reconstruction, and transformation can take place in given individuals. The individual child, youth, or adult is marked, and marked for life, by an administrator who will not bother to look twice to see who this individual actually is or how he is now related to the society of which he is a part. Personality configurations then must not be taken as static. They must be taken as indicative of ways in which the individual can develop and ways in which we may work with him to provide the experiences through which he may come into full and abundant Christian living.

We can do something of the same kind of analysis for groups. Conditions within society, conditions in the local community, and conditions within the families of our parishes make a vital difference in the kind of personality configuration that a group takes on. Very little has been done in the analysis of the " personalities " of groups.

This is a field in which the church school teacher might well become interested because of the make-up of the groups with which he or she is likely to deal. The ordinary church school teacher is not going to spend an inordinate amount of time on work with individuals as individuals. He is going to see and work with them in groups and classes. If this be the case, then certainly he might well take time to study the make-up of his group to discover what kind of persons are within the group and the ways in which their varying personalities react to and respond to one another.

One teacher, for instance, will discover that he has a group who come from many different parts of the community, the members attending so many different schools that they have no cohesiveness and no feeling of being a group. The members may have to spend a great deal of time vying with one another to discover who the natural leaders are and to establish status and role within the group. This is often a very difficult situation for the teacher to handle, because he seldom knows what is going on, and merely interprets all this behavior as disorder. He feels that he has an unruly group, a group who have to be managed, and does not see that because of the backgrounds from which the children came it is very difficult for them to get used to one another. It will take time for them to establish themselves as a group.

In another case a teacher may find that he has a group who come from one particular neighborhood. They know each other already. They all go to school together and have many interests and concerns in common that he may know nothing of. He may feel, therefore, that they are organized very compactly, but organized in a way against him, because he is not in on the things that they are interested in, that they are talking about, and that they are concerned with.

Certainly no teacher can be so carefully trained and so carefully prepared that he can teach *any* group, regardless of its experience and internal structure, with equal facility without knowing that group and how it is made up. This is why we speak of the necessity of discovering something of the personality configuration of the group with which we are to work.

Brief mention should be made again at this point of the fact that in the study of the nature and needs of the pupil it is very important to discover the distinctive nature and needs of our pupils within their community setting. There are great variations throughout the country, to say nothing of variations throughout the world, in the ways in which children, youth, and adults grow up and behave within their communities. Going from one region of the country to another, it is easy to see that conditions in various communities are quite different. This makes it very difficult to generalize on the nature and needs of pupils, and to plan for them so far as the curriculum is concerned.

When a careful study of the nature and needs of the pupil

has been made, general objectives may be interpreted in specific terms. No teacher or leader should ever approach a group of children, youth, or adults having in his mind only the general objectives of Christian education. No, he must interpret these objectives in terms of his particular group, its age level, its particular interests, and its particular level of achievement. He must interpret the general objectives in very concrete terms, stating specifically what the objectives are to be for a particular Sunday, a particular weekday session, or a particular vacation school session.

This he will do, if he is a wise teacher, in co-operation with the pupil. He will not plan for the pupil without taking him into active partnership. The beginning of the relationship between teacher and pupil in Christian education is the formulation of some specific objective or set of objectives that will guide the experiences through which they are to go together.

CURRICULUM, CONTENT, AND METHODS

On the basis of its general objectives, the study of the nature and needs of the pupil, and the statement of carefully developed objectives of a specific character, the process of Christian education moves into another area, the area of planning for curriculum, content, and methods.

The curriculum of Christian education has been defined as all those planned experiences by which the pupil becomes Christian.

Basically four processes are involved in the curriculum of Christian education. There is the process of guided study, in which materials and thought are united in intellectual exploration of the faith and its relationships to every facet of human life.

There is the process of fellowship, involving recreation. Many think of fellowship and recreation merely as processes of letting down after serious thought has been done or serious work accomplished. Actually the mood and atmosphere of fellowship and the activities of recreation are very important preconditions

for coming to certain Christian ideas and certain generalizations
about experience. It is very often only in the experience of fellowship or recreation that we come to realize that we can trust
the people with whom we are associated. It is in these experiences that we understand that these are persons with whom we
can think and work together. The mood and atmosphere of
working together is often created in the process of playing
together.

There is the process of social action. Social action is the area
in which we take our generalizations and convictions about the
Christian life into everyday life and try them out. This is the
proving and testing ground for our ideas. This is the place where
we discover the extent to which we have really grasped the truth
of the ideas with which we are dealing. The experiences that
we have in social action and in social service may be brought
back into the group with whom we are working, and with whom
we are thinking through the Christian faith, there to be rethought and possibly changed. There these experiences become
in turn resources for new ideas.

The curriculum procedures also include worship. When we
have arrived at certain basic convictions, when together we have
experienced deeply the things of the spirit, when we have come
to new awareness of God and his will for our life, and when we
have discovered something of who Christ was and what he is
for us today, then in meditation, in contemplation, and in common celebration we take our experiences, our convictions, and
our ideas together into the experience of deep and profound
worship. Worship becomes not just ceremony or ritual, not just
routine. It becomes the culminating experience of all of Christian education, an experience in which we learn the most integral and profound things about the Christian life. It is the experience in which we meet with the most real aspects of all our
group relationships, in which we see ourselves most clearly, and
in which the nature, the will, and the purpose of God become
manifest to us.

Curriculum implies content. The content that we will use is

as broad as human experience itself. But this is not enough to say, for we must apply some selective criteria in order to know what kind of content to use at various points. We will develop a general idea, worked out in some concrete detail, of the kind of content that is indispensable to the educated and mature Christian. We will then introduce this content at various points in the process. In doing so we will use two basic principles: the principle of grading and the principle of specificity.

The content that we use must be graded in such fashion that it will be challenging and stimulating to the child, the youth, or the adult, at his own level of achievement. But it must not be so challenging and stimulating that it is impossible of achievement and thus a source of frustration. Life holds enough thwarting experiences; we do not have to inject them into the planned curriculum. Content will be carefully selected in terms of the principle of grading in order that it may be challenging enough to help the pupil to take the next desirable step in his development.

The second principle to be used in the selection of content is the principle of specificity. Specific content will be chosen to meet the pupil's known interests and needs. We will not use a particular item of content simply because it has always been used before in the process. If we use it, it will be because it is specifically applicable to his needs, interests, and concerns at this time.

The principle of specificity also means that the specific knowledge, skill, or attitude to be learned will be included in the content and planned curriculum. If habits of Bible study are to be learned, the Bible will be studied. If techniques of Christian social action are to be learned, action will be planned and undertaken. If the pupil is to learn to worship, he will engage in experiences of worship. Discussion and study *about* these are not enough.

This will result, of course, in a great deal of adaptation of existing curriculum materials. At the same time it will help to guide in the selection of new materials that will go into

the printed curriculums. The content selected depends upon the
needs and experiences of the pupil in the development of the
Christian life. Bearing in mind at all times that everything that
we do ought to contribute to the development of the Christian
life, our content will be selected accordingly.

It is implied in this that there will be a great deal of content
in Christian education and that it will be rich. Christian education has used too little content. It has explored too few of the
relevant aspects of human experience, and those too superficially.
It has not penetrated deeply enough into the lives and experiences of the pupils to come to grips with them where they
really are.

The secret of content is twofold. The content must tap the
real experiences of the pupil in such a way that he is impressed
with its practicality for him and his concerns. It must introduce
him to new material, new experience, new content of a sort that
will enable him to become fascinated with the unexplored possibilities in the Christian faith and life.

Considerations of curriculum and content precede considerations of method. What are methods for? Methods are tools for
the accomplishment of our purposes. The curriculum tells us
what experiences are necessary. The content defines for us the
kind of materials we will use and the bases upon which we will
proceed; it gives us the richness and the fullness of our educational process. But neither of these answers the question of how
these experiences shall be introduced into the life of the pupil,
or how the content is to be used.

Methods have an integrity of their own. We cannot say that
any method that will achieve our immediate ends is to be used,
for there are many methods that in the long run discourage the
achievement of the Christian life. But in general we think of
methods as relative to the objectives and outcomes that we and
the pupils have in mind. They are relative in the sense that we
choose from a rich variety of possibilities those methods which
are most suitable for doing at any given time what is to be done.

Of late years there has been a great deal of discussion of the

relative merits of transmissive and creative methods in Christian
education. The choice between them is an unnecessary one.
Christian educators can know clearly what is to be transmitted
or communicated to the child, the youth, and the adult. Usually
the method that will be used will be one in which the individual
and the group re-create the experience. The very process of discovery or rediscovery, the process of making or remaking, the
process of creating or re-creating, is what we mean by creative
method. The materials of instruction usually associated with
transmissive education are just as useful as background for creative experience as they are for the kind of education for which
they were originally designed.

People who are interested in transmissive education are afraid
that the children, young people, and adults who are led into
creative education will not be introduced to the normative
standards of the Christian faith, and that they will not necessarily come out with conclusions that agree with those normative
standards. It has been a failing of a great deal of education that
calls itself creative that it has ignored the standards of the Christian faith. This is a mistake. To isolate the pupil from these
most important aspects of human experience is to make him forever the poorer.

On the other hand, the concern for the possibility that the
outcomes may not be in accord with Christian standards is one
of the problems that is almost insoluble. Christian education that
is creative is not the only kind of education that fails to guarantee its results. No kind of education can guarantee its results,
however conscientiously it sets out to achieve them. Look, for
instance, at transmissive education itself. Churches and church
schools conscientiously using transmissive methods have often
had to admit failure. The people who come through the process,
be it transmissive or creative, are not going to become Christian
inevitably as a result.

There is an even more profound aspect of the discussion of
transmissive and creative methodology. The very process of becoming Christian is itself a creative process: something new

takes place; something new comes into being. We talk about becoming Christian as a rebirth; we talk of the persons who have become Christian as new creatures. Rebirth cannot take place, at least rebirth that involves intelligent espousal of the Christian faith, without a background of knowledge of what the Christian faith means. But the Christian rebirth, dependent as it usually is upon the transmission of the Christian faith and Christian doctrine, is primarily a matter of the re-creation of human experience into experience that is divinely redeemed.

ORGANIZATION, ADMINISTRATION, SUPERVISION, AND EVALUATION

The Christian education program must be organized, administered, supervised, and evaluated with careful planning throughout in order to be at all successful. The best curriculum, the most thoroughgoing content, the most advanced and useful methods, used with careful knowledge of the pupil and careful adaptation of objectives to his nature and needs, can fall short if the program is not carefully and conscientiously organized, administered, supervised, and evaluated.

The organization of Christian education must take account of the total educational experience of every child, youth, and adult within the constituency of the church. Too long we have thought of the church school as the only aspect of our organized Christian education work. Actually our Christian education includes the church school, the weekday church school, the youth groups that meet under the sponsorship of the church (including youth fellowships, scouts, and other informal clubs), and the vacation church school. Occasionally a local church will also conduct its own camps and conferences. This is being expanded even more to include the necessity for some kind of organized approach not only within the church but within the home and the community as well.

When we think of the Christian education program thus broadly in terms of the whole experience of the child, and the way in which that experience may be organized in order that his life may become Christian, we have some grasp of what organization means. Whether or not we divide the church school into departments, the kind of classes we have, etc., are important questions. But they are not so important as the over-all question of organization: How is the church to organize to do its Christian education job for every individual, for his complete experience, for every age and experience level?

Once the organization has been set up, administration functions to make the wheels go around. Administration sees to it that the organization of Christian education operates smoothly and accomplishes what it is set up to do.

What leaders shall we have? Shall we have a director of Christian education? Shall we have a general superintendent and departmental superintendents? What is the minister's role?

How will the whole program be co-ordinated? Will we have a local church committee on Christian education? Will the teachers form themselves into a faculty group that will co-ordinate, or shall the co-ordination be done by an over-all body representative of the total educational interests of the church?

How shall the program of Christian education in its beyond-the-local-church aspects be administered and co-ordinated? What functions shall be handled by presbyteries, local conferences, or local associations? How shall they administer their program so that it will supplement and enrich the program of the local church?

Supervision is implied in administration. Supervision is the process of improving the teaching of religion. Another way of saying this is that all those activities and enterprises in which we seek to make the program better encompass the area of supervision.

Who does the supervision? Usually if there is a director of Christian education, this is his most important job. However, supervision may be done by the pastor, by the general superintendent, by the department superintendents, or by others specially designated to do it. In the best situations supervision is done on a co-operative basis by all these persons working together.

Supervision includes the training of leaders. Leadership training schools, as well as more informal types of activities, are part
of the process. The "workshop" method of leadership training
has been experimented with lately and is proving to be especially
interesting and useful.

Supervision implies that those who do the supervising have an
over-all idea of what the program of Christian education ought
to be, rooted in a mature idea of the Christian life and the way
growth in the Christian life takes place.

The supervisor must in a sense know the total area that he is
concerned with, and must be able to see the individual teacher's
problems and achievements in light of the total job that is to be
done. He is, therefore, the person who will constantly keep the
general objectives in mind and help to formulate the specific
objectives. He observes what is going on, and helps the teacher
and leader to do their jobs better. Supervision may include supervision of classroom teaching, informal activities, recreation,
worship, or any other aspect of the program.

Results should be forthcoming. The most important will be
those results that accrue in the life of the individual pupil, the
degree to which he achieves the aims of Christian education in
his own life, and the extent to which he becomes Christian. We
ought to make periodic, but not constant, checkups on our results. When we have some fairly clear idea of the results that
we have been able to achieve, we can use methods of testing and
evaluation to discover the extent to which our specific objectives
have been reached and the extent to which the general objectives
of Christian education have been attained in the individual, the
church, the family, the community, and society at large. Plans
for the next steps may then be made intelligently.

What has been said in this analysis of the process of Christian
education may seem to be unduly organizational. On careful
scrutiny it will be seen that this is not the case. The process of
Christian education when analyzed is seen to include only the
essential means to be used to lead the child, the youth, or the

adult to the place where God may take hold of his life, that he may live the life in Christ and grow into its mature fullness.

The process of Christian education has an integrity in itself. If this were not true, then another could be better substituted for it. But it has become obvious over the years that Christian education is needed if the Church is to live and if the individual in our society is to come to fullness of life in Christ.

The experience that we have had with Christian education indicates that with all the careful planning that must go into it, and all the individual and group stewardship involved, the aims that it seeks to achieve are so much more significant and important than any of its processes, or all of its processes taken together, that the process becomes relative to and flexible within the context of its aims.

It must not be regarded as static and fixed. It must rather be thought of as the best that we have achieved up to this time. We must seek so to improve it and to change it that it will be ever more effective. Christian education is a matter of service to the individual, to society, to the Church, and to God. To the extent that it serves its purpose it is good; if need be, it must be reconstructed that it may serve its purpose better.

Part Two

THE LIFE IN CHRIST

Chapter 4

RELIGION IS NOT ENOUGH

DISCOVERING AND LIVING the Christian life is the task of Christian education. The Christian educator seeks the reconstruction and transformation of personality, the reconstruction and transformation of his own personality and those of the children, youth, and adults with whom he lives and works, that they may together come to the fullness of the Christian life.

REDISCOVERY OF RELIGION

There is in this country at present a rediscovery of religion. More and more people are becoming interested in religion, finding its power, and using it in order to develop for themselves a poised, calm, and creative way of living. They are finding in it the power to meet certain situations that have troubled and baffled them. We hear people who a few years ago would never have thought of speaking of religion in a positive or constructive fashion now commenting quite favorably upon it. However, if we press them far enough, we are likely to discover that they are interested only in a kind of personal faith that does wonderful things for them and that they feel can do the same for other people, but that has little connection in their minds either with traditional Christianity or with the organized Christian Church. Religion is advocated today in many books and lectures; there is comment on it over the radio and on television; it is discussed in college classrooms; but it is often divorced from distinctive relationship to the Christian faith or the Church.

Religion is something of a universal reality in human life.

43

There is scarcely any nation, people, or tribe that does not have a recognizable religion. As a mater of fact, persons who disavow having any particular religion do not mean that they do not have religious experience. They mean as a rule that they do not participate in or support organized religion. Of course they hold values and have faith, but may mistakenly not recognize these as being indicators of their real religion. Broadly speaking, religion is something that people have and do wherever they exist. The religious quest is one of the important and necessary aspects of human life wherever human life is found.

RELIGION IN HUMAN LIFE

How does religion function in human life? It draws together those aspects of life that have value for the individual or for the group. It highlights and celebrates those aspects of life through which life may be lived to the full and the good life achieved. This may be said of any kind of religion. Certain values, ends, objectives, and goals are chosen and the person or group choosing them gives devotion and worship to them. Religion functions to develop commitment on the part of the individual or the group to those values and truths by which the individual or the group may live.

A most distinctive thing about religion, however, is the way in which in society it is broken up, the way in which it divides peoples and groups throughout the world. A number of religions have through the centuries come into existence, flourished, and died. Other religions, some ancient and some fairly recent, have come into existence and flourish even now. It would appear that most religions rise and fall with the civilizations they represent. There is a kind of correspondence between the values that a civilization holds and its religion, so that as the civilization dies the religion is also likely to die.

As we look around the world and into history at this plurality of religions, it is possible for us to get an objective view of what religion is and how it functions. Coming home, we discover that in our country there is more of a plurality of religious experience, even though most of it derives from and is gathered up within the Jewish-Christian tradition, than may be found in any other nation anywhere in the world. Almost every other nation has something more of a homogeneity of religious experience and religious organization than we have.

This plurality of religious experience in our country is one of our persistent concerns. We in the United States are tempted to minimize our religious differences. We live next door to people of different faiths; it is just as well to keep peace in the neighborhood. But, however laudable may be the movements to minimize the differences between the various faiths in this country, it must be recognized that there are differences that cannot be minimized without destroying the faith's integrity. It is well to look with interest, understanding, and appreciation upon our neighbor's faith, but that interest, understanding, and appreciation must not be allowed to minimize the importance, centrality, and truth of our own faith. In order to live a rich and creative life together in this country we must highlight the riches of our various faiths, each of us living his faith to the full, not letting the temptation to minimize the differences minimize the faiths instead.

The attitude that religion, broadly speaking, is enough and that you do not have to go beyond a vague sort of personal, intimate, and individual religious experience is symptomatic of minimizing the differences at the expense of the faith. The idea that religion is enough is heralded by this kind of statement: "It does not matter what you believe so long as you believe it with your whole heart and act upon it." How can such a statement be made in good conscience today? Mussolini took over Italy; Hitler took over Germany; their beliefs brought on World War II. Communism, a form of belief that turns belief inside out, has become a force in Russia and throughout the greater part of the world, producing misery and terror. It matters terribly what we believe; the most crucial thing in the world is what we believe. There are altogether too many demonstrations before our eyes of what happens when we believe the wrong thing, when we believe what is not true, and when we believe in that which is unjust, unrighteous, and diabolical, producing hate rather than love.

Religion is not enough; faith is not enough; personal feelings of quietude, poise, and integration are not enough. They are enough only when they are set within a context of Christian truth, Christian righteousness, and Christian love. The fallacy in thinking that religion is enough becomes apparent when we see its results.

It results in delusion about the importance of the nature and destiny of human life. When we say religion is enough, we say that various theories of the nature and destiny of human life are relatively insignificant; we refuse to espouse any one theory of its nature and destiny. When we thus delude ourselves, we are casting out to sea with no rudder, no compass, and no pilot.

It results in our cutting ourselves off from the resources of the Christian life. When we say that religion without Christ and without the Church is enough, we cease to pray, to worship, to engage in Bible study, and to fellowship together with those who are seeking righteousness, truth, and love in Christ. In this we are cutting ourselves off from the resources of the Christian life; we are cutting ourselves off from the resources of life itself.

As Protestants and as Christians we may aver that religion is enough, saying, " To each man his own religion." But this may well result in our becoming responsible for letting unchristian forces loose in the world. Minimizing our own religion is likely to result in our losing faith in it and ceasing to be loyal followers. But other people do not lose faith in the values that they espouse; other people do not lose faith in the things to which they have committed themselves. What we are doing is to weaken those things in which we believe and upon which our life depends, and on the other hand to strengthen opposing forces.

It results in the denial of the spiritual bases for our common life. We do not live by bread alone; we do not live by technology alone; we do not live by vague notions of what is good and true. It was not thus that our country was built; it was not thus that our civilization has come to the point where it can support and encourage the values by which we live and that we seek to re-create in the lives of our children. It is chiefly by the things of the spirit that we have come to this point. If we deny the validity of Christian righteousness, Christian truth, and Christian love, we are denying those spiritual foundations which undergird our common life.

We may escape these results because we have absorbed the values of the Christian life in part at least by growing up in an atmosphere permeated with Christian faith. It may have become a part of our unconscious existence, and we will continue to live by its values of morality and spirituality even while with our lips we are denying the validity of their sources. But our children will not thus escape. We may be able to ride out the denial of the spiritual bases of our common life, but our children will reap the whirlwind that we have sown. At the present time we are, as a matter of fact, witnessing the reaping of the whirlwind in some aspects of our life, one that was sown by the very denial of the spiritual bases of our common life in a former generation.

In the Gospels there is a telling instance of the denial of the specific validity of Christ and his truth. If we deny his validity and truth, saying that religion is enough without him, without the church, and without the faith, we will also, as it were, hear the cry of the cock as dawn breaks, and we will have the same inner feeling of lostness, the same kind of remorse, that Peter must have felt after he had denied his Lord.

THE CHRISTIAN FAITH

Looking at the Christian faith directly, what are its essentials? We believe in an incarnate, risen, and living Lord and Redeemer. We believe in a faith and way of righteousness, truth, and love. We believe in the supreme reality of the triune God: the Father, gracious and almighty; Jesus Christ, his only Son, the living Word and the living Lord; and the Holy Spirit, ever-present, motivating and guiding.

There was that little group of men, discouraged, alone, and utterly defeated, out of whom at Pentecost the Church was born because this faith was their faith, and because a faith like this could not be denied, nor its power destroyed. It was this faith that was the basis of their life together; it is still the basis of our Christian life together. Out of this simple and concrete faith — there is nothing particularly abstract about it — came the creeds, definitions of the faith, to which we give allegiance, and the organization and fellowship of the Church, at first weak in numbers but strong in spirit, then great in numbers and great in spirit.

It was by nature a catholic faith, universal, and with worldwide validity. Here it began to become catholic in its spread throughout the known world. It became somewhat weakened in the first attempt to make it catholic since it tended to compromise itself and its leadership in return for official sanction of its existence. Nevertheless something of its later fulfillment was hinted at at that time as it became the religion of the Roman Empire.

Creative and definitive thinking about the Church, its faith and its life, took place during the first centuries of its life. A man like Saint Augustine symbolizes its spiritual and intellectual strength. Through endless explorations of byways, reluctance to forego the satisfactions of paganism, and consequent overlong hesitation, he became a Christian and finally the most thoroughgoing and influential Christian thinker of his day. His exposition of doctrine and his clear vision of the role of faith in the world as the " City of God " stand for all time as monuments of Christian realism.

The Church, with the collapse of the Roman Empire, moved into a period in which it alone maintained the unity of society. The men who preached the gospel in those days may often not have understood it, but had they not continued to preach, teach, and read its truth, the gospel of the love of God in Christ possibly would not have been born again as it was into a new and reborn world. One of the miracles of God in history is the way men kept saying the words in those threatening years, while the faith remained dormant and obscure, lacking vitality and in need of renewal.

The time came, in the Age of Faith, when the words did mean something again. The great flowering of faith in the late Middle Ages, the time of Saint Thomas Aquinas and the time of the building of the great cathedrals, saw Christian truth gloriously developed in its philosophical, theological, and artistic aspects. The Age of Faith broke down only when the faith had been spun out to the place where it was no longer the faith of the common man.

It experienced another rebirth in the Renaissance and the Reformation, a rebirth and renewal of individual expression, individual faith, and individual responsibility. In the Renaissance its individualism was that of art and the spirit. In the Reformation its individualism was that of responsibility, cleanliness, purity, and primitive simplicity in religion.

With the Reformation came the founding of our particular Protestant tradition in the history of the Church. But we do not think of it as the founding of our tradition; we think of it as a reannouncing of the principles that had been fundamental in Christ's ministry and in the Early Church but that had been lost along the way. The Reformation did not so much see the formation of new churches, as the re-formation of the Church of Jesus Christ in something more like its original and primitive form. The two principles that the Reformation brought again to man's attention were those of the supremacy of the Word and justification by faith. Justification by faith means justification by what we are rather than by anything we may be able or may choose to do, justification in terms of the qualities that by grace are within us and not in terms of anything we can earn by extraneous means.

Following the Reformation there came a period in which liberalism grew. The presuppositions of political and economic liberalism were in certain ways an affirmation and in others a denial of the traditional Christian faith. Yet we even now live with these original presuppositions and the propositions of economic and political liberalism. Among them is that God has created this universe to operate by law and has created man good. We believe this — it is the Christian faith. However, also among its propositions is that society and social controls stifle the good and that the good has only to be released within man, by eliminating social controls, to come to full fruition. This we cannot as Christians believe. To the extent that this has crept into our politics, our economics, and our education we must criticize them, for they deny what our faith teaches about the nature of man, society, and sin. If we merely think of the flowering of human nature in terms of the unfolding of what is within, our thought cannot lead to the profound, rich, and real experiences of God, nature, and man that give meaning to the Christian life.

At the present time there are four threats to Protestantism with which we have to deal: the threat of radical old-fashioned liberalism of the type of rugged individualism just described; the threat of what might be called neutralism, that is, the idea of watering down the faith until it becomes a thing without any color, indistinguishable, and lacking in truth; the threat of nationalistic paganism, to a certain extent in this country but for the most part in other parts of the world; and the threat of Communistic humanism. These are counterfaiths, counterreligions, that we shall let loose in this world if we tend to minimize the faith that is within us as Protestant Christians.

Christian history is a record of faith. It tells of a people who lived by faith. It tells of a Saviour who lived the perfect life of faith, who died and rose again that faith might be established in this world forever. It tells us how we today may have a faith that overcomes the world.

Christianity is a living religion, a living faith, that centers all of life upon the dominant purpose to do the will of God and to live in Christ. Religion that is not Christian is not enough.

Chapter 5

A FAITH TO BE TAUGHT

CHRISTIAN EDUCATION has for years been aware of the controversy between an educational theory that emphasizes subject matter and one that emphasizes the experience of the pupil. The dispute has been raging for many years in general educational circles and has been seriously reflected in Christian education.

We have been told that education takes place as the experience of the learner expands and is refined and directed, and that the most effective education takes place at points of deepest concern in the pupil's experience. Accordingly, all of education should begin and take direction from hints that come from the experience of the pupil himself.

This is important and true for Christian education, but exclusive emphasis on this aspect of education has caused Christian educators serious concern.

With a clear conception of what the Christian faith is, they hope it may become the property of children and youth, and of those adults who have not already been made aware of it.

We cannot be satisfied unless the Christian faith is learned, and we feel that there are definite propositions, definite content, and definite subject matter in the Christian faith that must be thus learned. We are also deeply concerned about starting always with pupil experience; we are haunted by the feeling that possibly if we use this approach too consistently the child or youth will not be introduced to all the necessary aspects of the Christian faith. This is still a plaguing question in Christian education, and one that has to be dealt with quite forthrightly.

THREE PRINCIPLES FOR DEALING WITH CONTENT
AND EXPERIENCE

It is a question, however, that need not plague us so seriously as it has. For it is very possible for us to use the experience of the pupil — it is possible for us to use *our* experience as learners in the Christian life — and at the same time be assured that we shall not miss the riches and the fullness of Christian truth and the Christian faith. In order to effect this combination of subject matter and experience, content and experience, in one unified concept in education, three principles are necessary. Within these the groundwork may be laid for a consideration of what the Christian faith is in relation to Christian education.

The first principle is that experience for any human being is continuous. It is untrue to our nature to think of our lives as having thoroughly separate stages of development that we call early childhood, middle childhood, late childhood, early adolescence, middle adolescence, late adolescence, young adulthood, maturity, and old age. Of course we go through these periods, but the more important thing for us is that as we go through them we go through them as persons whose experience is continuous. We think of ourselves as ourselves rather than as children, youth, or adults. It is less real for me to say, " I am an adult," than it is for me to say, " I am myself."

The experience of the people with whom we are working in education is continuous experience; they have a real consciousness of self. They are looking for new experience, for guidance, and for personal enrichment within that continuous experience. It is false for us to think that experience is broken up into little segments and that we deal with people in radically different fashion at distinct points on the developmental scale. We do deal with them in different fashion at various points, but we deal with them primarily as persons whose experience is continuous.

This means that when the individual comes to a point where he says, " Now I am a Christian," what has happened is that a long period of experience, continuous in character, has led to the place where his life has taken on a new orientation, focus, and center. It is so new and radically different that he knows himself to be a renewed or reborn person. Yet he maintains identity with his past experience. He is himself, but now he is himself in Christ. Thus the principle of the continuity of experience operates even in the most important of Christian experiences.

The second principle upon which we may found a theory for dealing with content and experience is that the development of personality takes place through experience. We do not develop personality in a vacuum. We develop it only as we as organisms, minds, and spirits feel the forces around us that impinge upon our lives, and as we respond to them. As little children, we respond to the mother and the father. As children growing up, we respond to our playmates, our friends, our teachers, and other leaders. Our responses expand as our experience expands.

The time comes when within our experience the reality of God becomes a central reality, and we experience response to him. Our personalities become Christian through a growing, expanding, changing, transforming, and reconstructing experience. The best way to describe the Christian life is to describe it in terms of Christian experience. When we describe it thus, we are simply enunciating in another fashion this same principle. If experience is continuous and if personality develops through experience, it becomes of the utmost importance that we pay careful heed to the kinds of experience that come to influence children, youth, and adults, and that come to influence us.

Thus we come to the third principle that brings into focus the matter of subject matter or content. This is the principle of the guidance and enrichment of experience. It is at this point that the question of the faith appears as a live issue.

Let us look at this term. We talk about faith, and we talk about *the* faith. Here is one word that we use with two different meanings, which are yet so interlocked that together they give us a picture of what the Christian life is in its experiential setting and in its setting as a body of content.

Faith is the experience that we have of whole response to the call and to the guidance of God. Faith is the quality that experience takes on when life is lived in Christ. When we talk about the possibility and necessity of growing in faith, we mean growth in Christian experience. At the same time, when we talk about *the* faith or *a* faith, we mean a set of propositions, a set of beliefs, a set of teachings, a set of doctrines, or a set of dogmas that are essentially intellectual definitions of the basis for the experience that we call faith. The meanings of the term are thus interlocked and intertwined; they make one picture for us within the Christian life.

It must be said that the Christian life in the last analysis does not depend upon an exhaustive intellectual analysis or an intellectual assent to a set of doctrinal propositions. Christ in calling human beings calls each one in terms of that person's experience and ability to respond. There are those who cannot respond except at a level that combines with all the other factors in personality a keen necessity for complete intellectual response. Many cannot answer the call of Christ without thinking through very carefully who it is that is calling them, what it is he is calling them to, and what it means for all the aspects of their lives. We therefore, if we are of a philosophical or a theological turn of mind, must have a thoroughgoing idea of, and assent to, the Christian faith as part of our commitment.

But there are those who do not think philosophically or theologically. Christ does not turn us away if our personalities and our lives are such that they are not thus oriented. A man may become a man in Christ at the point where he recognizes that Christ is the very center of meaning for his life. It does not necessarily mean that he has to understand every proposition in the catechism; it does not necessarily mean that he has to digest a confession of faith; it does not necessarily mean that he has to answer deep and profound theological questions. No, the basic experience of the Christian faith is the experience of personal response to One who lives and ever lives, in whom life itself is revealed to us.

This is not to say that our experience and our response are to be nonintellectual, nor is it to say that the faith is unimportant. Certainly not. It does mean that Christ calls each one of us at his own level of ability to respond. It is important for us as Christian educators to remember that he calls the person who is unable to respond at a profound level of intellectual understanding. It is just as important for us to remember that he calls each individual at his *most* profound level of understanding and ability to respond. We should take full cognizance of the fact that Christ calls our pupils and that he calls us thus deeply at the center of what we can be. Christ knows what we must be, and it is at the point of what we must be in him that he calls us.

These basic experiences of the Christ lead to the place where education can be education for the life in Christ. For most of us it will include a thoroughgoing analysis of and commitment to the Christian faith as doctrine, as teaching, and as a definitive formulation of what the life in Christ is.

Content and subject matter are then necessities in the process of Christian education. They are important to us as teachers and leaders, for we are not equipped unless each of us at his own level of ability to respond has mastered the essential content. Every teacher has had the experience of discovering that in teaching he for the first time has learned things that he thought he had known all along. He has the amazing experience of finding out that he learns more than his pupils learn, even though he is supposed to be the teacher and they the learners. The teacher and leader must seek at every point to master the essential content.

At the same time it is essential to recognize that the content and subject matter of the Christian faith must at every point be graded: graded to pupil need, graded to pupil capacity, graded to pupil interest — in a word, graded to the readiness of the pupil to respond. This is one of the reasons why it is so important for the teacher to know well every child in his class or every young person in his group. If we do not know our children and young people as individuals, how can we go about the process of grading subject matter and experiences to their need, capacity, and interest? If the teacher gives them a chance to be known, they will make themselves known, and the teacher will have some clue as to how to grade the material to the point where there is active need, real capacity, and urgent interest.

What the Christian Educator Teaches

The matter of *the* faith is not to be neglected in Protestantism. The daughter in a Protestant family had been reared in church and church school. In time she married a young man whose heritage was also Protestant. They went to live in one of the large Protestant cities in this country. Looking for a church home, it was said that they shopped for a religion. They went from church to church, from minister to minister, asking, " What does your church teach, and what does it offer to a young couple like us just starting out together? " As a result, they joined the Roman Catholic Church, the only Church where they felt they had found a clear account of what the Church taught.

This is a scandal, that we should leave people who are eagerly seeking a faith, eagerly seeking the Christian faith, thus in the dark and not be alert to explain to them in convincing terms what the Church teaches.

Christianity is a faith to be understood and a faith to be taught. As we teach the Christian faith, what are we teaching? Often we do not realize what breadth there is to the thing that we are trying to do in making clear this intellectual basis for the Christian life.

We are teachers of history. The Bible is a book of history. It is hard to be historically accurate in dealing with the Bible; nevertheless it is important that Bible teaching be historical in character and that it seek ever greater accuracy. We have to make it plain how the Bible came to be, how the life of the Hebrew people developed, and how their ideas of God developed. We have to be clear as to what it meant that at a particular point of readiness in Hebrew history and in the history of the world, Christ, God incarnate, became a reality in history. We must teach Christ as real in history at the point where he was the Jesus of history,

and as a reality in history antedating that point and postdating
that point as the living Christ, the living Word. We must think
very clearly about the concept of God working in and through
history. We must be intelligent about the history of the Christian
Church, the development of the faith in the historical process.
We must know the relation between Christianity, the living
Christ, the Church, and the world at this point in history. We
must thus be profoundly historical in the teaching of the Christian faith.

We are teachers of literature. The Bible may be approached as
literature. It is of course more than just literature, but unless
we and our pupils understand it for its variety and its richness
of literary composition and quality we shall not be able accurately to comprehend what it is that God is saying through it.
If we do not recognize, for instance, that the psalms are particular forms of poetry, they are likely to remain obscure for us and
for our pupils. If we do not see that The Book of Job is a drama,
it will be very difficult for us to make it clear. If we do not understand that the first three Gospels are narrative biography and
that the Fourth Gospel is interpretative biography, the relationship becomes obscure.

At the same time, we are teachers of Christian literature since
Biblical times. We have to bring into focus the literary experience of the Christian life and the Christian Church throughout
the years in such form that our pupils will be able to grasp it.
This means, among other things, so to saturate ourselves with it
that it becomes our own intellectually.

We are teachers of the arts. The Christian truth and faith are
expressed in the arts. In music, in architecture, in painting, and
in the other arts, the Christian faith is interpreted and made
clearer. The creative artistic riches of the Christian past and
present are to be explored and appreciated. At the present time
there is an interesting renaissance in Christian music and art.
There is also a growing acceptance of creative methodology in
Christian education. The Christian faith becomes more lucid as
well as more applicable to each situation as we ourselves tell it

in a variety of ways and through a variety of artistic mediums.

We are teachers of philosophy at every point where we deal with beliefs about the ultimate nature of the universe; beliefs about the sources, validity, and uses of knowledge; and beliefs about basic values, beliefs in the fields of ethics, aesthetics, politics, and all the rest of the areas in which we develop value concerns. Not one class session goes by, nor one period of preparation for teaching, but we have to deal with one or more of these basic questions of philosophy.

We are teachers of theology. The most profound questions with which we have to deal are summed up in the systematic statement of our faith. We teach in order to develop an awareness of certain theological questions, and to make clear those propositions through which the Church seeks to answer them. We teach about God, his nature, and his relationship to his universe and to man.

Here is an aspect of the faith that illustrates why the teacher himself must master the essential content. He is at sea in trying to teach about God unless he knows what God's nature and works are. It is, however, not simply a matter of being clear ourselves about these things. Once we have developed personal clarity, then it may be possible for us to interpret, in words and experiences that the pupil will understand, those theological truths which must be conveyed within the Christian faith.

We have the task of teaching who man is in relation to God. What is he in the eyes of God? What was he originally? What has he become? Here the reality of sin as a theological and as a specific proposition becomes a question for us. How may we again become what God purposes for us? Here we consider grace and its operations in human life.

In the process of considering the nature of God and the nature of man it becomes imperative that we consider the person and work of Christ: who Christ was, who Christ is; what Christ did, and what he does now.

This involves clarity about the meaning of redemption, the work that Christ does with men, and the way in which grace operates in human life, not just in theory or in academic terms, but related at point after point to the experience of children, youth, and adults so that it may mean to them the possibility and reality of redemption.

We must teach the meaning and functions of the Church and the use of what we call the means of grace, by which an individual is aided in coming closer to the realities and fulfillment of the Christian life.

Among these profound and eternal questions we must deal with the question of last things. What is the ultimate end and hope of humanity? How is man's ultimate destiny in the eyes of God related to mine? What may I do within society to enable society to fulfill the purposes that God has in mind for it? How deeply this question affects society and our own personal lives! The question of last things becomes for us the question of our part in the fulfillment of God's purpose. What does he have in mind and what is my part in it? This is an imperative concern demanding clarity from us and our pupils.

It is a significant matter thus to be teachers of history, literature, the arts, philosophy, and theology. When we ourselves are intelligent in these fields, and when we have learned to express ourselves creatively and adequately in them, we shall be in a position to find out how we may lead others through them into an experience of the Christian life that has depth so far as content and subject matter are concerned. We as teachers must then master these essentials for the Christian life; we must become persons who through training and experience can grade these areas of subject matter and content accurately according to pupil readiness. When we have so mastered these things ourselves that they mean more than life itself to us, then there is a "running over the brim" that enables us to guide the lives of others in coming somewhat closer to a deep understanding and appreciation of what the Christian life and the Christian faith are. Our aim in the area of subject matter and content is the achievement of fullness of life in Christ through the guidance and enrichment of experience.

No one would expect the volunteer church school teacher or the ordinary parent to be expert in all these fields. They are listed here not to raise discouraging barriers, but for two purposes: to emphasize the undeniable fact of a rich and essential content without which Christian education is meaningless, and to challenge the Christian teacher to abandon superficiality in his faith and begin perhaps at some one point to develop proficiency in knowing and dealing with it.

Chapter 6

THE INDISPENSABLE BOOK

THE BIBLE is the indispensable book. The Revised Standard Version of the Bible became in its first year of publication the greatest best seller in the United States, with over two and one half million copies sold. The Bible in the King James Version has been for years the best seller in the English language. The Bible has been translated into so many tongues that there are very few peoples in the world to whom it is not available.

Yet if we are honest about it we will admit that for all its popularity, it is little known. We might say that it is the book most read and least understood. It is certainly a book that has been interpreted in most diverse fashion. It has given rise to more controversy, discord, and disagreement than any other outstanding book we know. Yet it is our only indispensable book.

OUR PROBLEMS AS TEACHERS AND STUDENTS OF THE BIBLE

What are some of the problems that teachers of the Bible face? Most of us who are engaged in Christian education are engaged in the Christian education of children and youth. We try to carry on Biblical education along with the other aspects of Christian education. In the process we are likely to forget that the Bible is primarily a book by and for adults. We treat it as if it were a children's book. We fail to give our children the experience appropriate to them, appreciation of it as a book that they must grow up to rather than a book that they may master during childhood, and then like most of the adults in their environment virtually ignore during adulthood. The Bible was written by people mature in the experience of the living God; the Bible is a book that opens itself up only to mature people. This does not mean at all that we are to keep it away from children, but it does mean that we regard it essentially as a book by adults and for adults. We do not ever regard the task as accomplished when we have taught children the Bible at the level of a child's understanding.

The Bible is a book whose teachings are profound. In many places these teachings are not easy to grasp, even in the clearest translations. Yet we mistreat the Bible and misrepresent it by oversimplification. We try to give our students in a nutshell what cannot be reduced to a nutshell, saying that we try to give them an over-all picture of the Bible. We actually leave out so much essential material that it is impossible to grasp what the book is about and what it is trying to teach; we leave out huge sections, notably the Prophets, that are absolutely essential to an understanding of what the Bible's message is in its comprehensiveness and completeness.

The Bible is the revelation of God to men, and as such is the record of the history of man's grasp of the truth that is revealed. We misrepresent the Bible if we teach that every part of it is equally important. There is a basic principle for the interpretation of the Bible. This principle is the relevance of Christ to the entire Biblical epic, even to all history itself. The eternal Christ is the principle and norm of significance for the entire Bible; the Word made flesh in Jesus Christ is the center of the Biblical message. In the Bible that which is less than the full truth of Christ, or that which is peripheral to the truth of Christ, has to be interpreted in terms of the central meaning, Christ as the Word of God. This is a Christ-centered theory of Biblical interpretation, emphasizing the fact that men grew as God helped them to grow in their grasp of his revelation to them, and maintaining that the indispensable record of that growth is the Bible.

The Bible is primarily a book that contains religious insights; it is primarily a religious book. We mistreat it by using it as if it were a source book in geology or psychology, by using it as a blueprint for contemporary ethical practice, or by using it (and this is the worst misuse of the Bible) as a magical device for individual guidance. In order to see clearly for ourselves what it may mean for men, women, and children to be religious, the Bible is an indispensable source of religious truth. But it is not to be misused as a source book of some other kind.

These are plaguing problems to teachers of the Bible. They point directly to a theme that will recur in this chapter, that is, that the main difficulty in the case of many teachers of the Bible is that they do not know the Bible very well themselves. They do not grasp its central message; they are unable to interpret certain parts of it because they have not really studied them.

What sort of problems, then, do we have as students of the Bible? We do not apprehend the content of the Bible, nor do we know how to find out what is in it. The person who starts with the first chapter of Genesis to read the Bible chapter by chapter in order to get to know it will possess a great deal of stamina if he gets very far beyond the first few chapters of Leviticus. Chances are that he will bog down before he gets anywhere near what the Bible has most significantly to teach. If he does get to the heart of the Old Testament, the Prophets, he may find them so baffling, the allusions so far from his experience, that it is almost impossible for him to sustain interest, to say nothing of grasping their meaning. So he satisfies himself by picking out those few passages that he can understand, that speak to his spirit, and uses them exclusively, even thinking that he is a serious student of the Bible.

Teachers of the Bible must be students of the Bible, and know how to find out what is in it. They have to secure those source books and materials which will help them, those guides which will assist them to understand the backgrounds out of which the Bible grew and to which it has constant reference. Some teachers have peculiar difficulty even in dealing with the Gospels, since the names of various political and religious groups of the time are unfamiliar to them. A comparatively simple matter like the real differences between the Pharisees and the Sadducees is ignored, even though it is necessary to an understanding of the teachings of Jesus.

Even more important than the fact that we do not try to dig into and understand the Bible in its various portions is the fact that we do not comprehend its central meaning and purpose. Christians believe that there is one major purpose in the Bible, one essential story and message. We have been brought up on the fact that the Bible is a collection of books, written by many people at many different times; but we have often failed to discover and to convey the fact that the central theme of the whole Bible is the story of God and his relations with his people. There is no portion of the Bible that does not in some form or other shed light upon this central theme and message. The whole Bible is the story of God's speaking his word to man in a variety of ways, but climactically in Jesus Christ.

We do not take the trouble to find out how the Bible came into being. We do not try to discover the origins of its various parts. This leads us into great confusion because we are likely to take it for granted that the Bible is now arranged as it was originally written. The Bible as we now have it consists of editings of many earlier materials. We think, for instance, of the Prophets as coming late among Old Testament writings while there are actually few portions of the Old Testament writings that were not edited and re-edited to present the essential prophetic message that is their central theme.

We do not attempt to grasp the significance of the various parts of the Bible or the types of materials that are included in it. There are, for instance, portions of the Bible that are narrative in character. Is there some particular significance to the fact that portions of the Bible are written as stories or epics? Our God is a God who works in history; he works in the hearts of men in the historical process; therefore, it is important that many portions of the Bible were written, not in abstract terms, but in the concrete style of epics, stories, narrative, and biography, by which God is seen actually working in history in the lives of men.

Some portions of the Bible are philosophical; some consist of epigrammatic sayings; some contain sermons and other speeches; and some are written as letters guiding people in specific situations. Poetry and drama are included in the Bible. Some portions combine several of these types of literature. The materials of the Bible have been arranged and edited to make them clear and in order that they might express God's purpose accurately.

As students of the Bible, we suffer from the fact that we are the victims of our own teaching and its limitations. Many of us are teachers of the Bible to children. We teach the Bible on the child's level and run the danger as adults of understanding it in childish fashion. We are in danger of thinking of it primarily in terms of the stories that we tell to children, the verses that we have children memorize, or of the limited number of passages that we can and do use with little children.

We have to recognize that the amount of Biblical material that can thus be used is severely limited. It is necessarily limited in practice. Study the amount of the Bible that is used in Christian education at the present time or that has been used in times past in any curriculum or in any Christian education program and you begin to see how very limited in scope the use of the Bible is with children. But we as adults should certainly get beyond the point where we understand and think of the Bible in childish terms. Why do we lose our young people at the end of the junior high period, just at the point where the Bible could begin to be clear to them? Why do we lose them at the very point where it could be so stimulating and so challenging to them? The answer is clear: because we cannot ourselves seem to push beyond the limitations of our childish understanding of the book.

As students of the Bible we run into the problem of reading our own preconceptions into it. We think we know what the Bible is supposed to teach, or someone has told us convincingly what it is supposed to teach. As we read we do an unconsciously selective thing: we read into the Bible what we think ought to be there. This is arrogance in the matter of Bible study. If the Bible is the Word of God and if through the Bible God speaks to us, the thing for us to do is to listen to what he has to say, to listen with our whole mind, our whole heart, our whole understanding, and not try to talk back so loudly and so persistently that we cannot hear what he has to say to us. People who have done a very limited job of Bible study are often very ready to tell us what it is all about. Such persons are very likely to be closing their ears to what God has to say to them in it.

THE PLACE OF THE BIBLE IN CHRISTIAN TEACHING

On the positive side, what is the place of the Bible in Christian teaching? The Bible is a necessary part of the understanding and experience of the mature, informed, and intelligent Christian. It is essential to know, understand, and study it; this is Biblical education.

There is a distinction, however, between Christian education and Biblical education. The teaching of the Bible — information about the Bible or the contents of the Bible — is one important aspect, but only one, of Christian education. We come closest to what the Bible means for Christian education when we recognize that it is the Word of God and when we come into a personal relationship of listening to what the Word is, or trying to understand what God is saying to us in his Word. This is a very personal and experiential thing. Christian education is centrally concerned with the experience of becoming a man, a woman, a young person, a child in Christ.

If our entire aim were to know the Bible and understand it, but we did not make its message personally and experientially ours, then we should be doing less than Christian education. This is the essential distinction between Biblical education, which is teaching about the Bible, and Christian education, which is the process of becoming a person in Christ. The Bible is an indispensable aid and resource in a process that is emphatically experiential.

However, the Bible is more. It is a norm, a standard, for the values to be taught in Christian education. In judging and developing character, how shall we choose between the various values that present themselves as possible standards? In developing a point of view and practice in Christian education, how shall we choose between the various values upon which we might base our thought and action? The standards by which we choose are those values which the Bible clearly teaches. It is essential in Christian education to concentrate upon those values which are centrally Biblical. The values are quite clear: justice, righteousness, truth, and love. The Bible, because it insists upon and teaches these things, becomes the norm for the values to be taught and used in Christian education.

Furthermore, the Bible is a guide to a way of life that is fundamentally Christian. How could one adopt and develop a Christian way of life without making the Bible his own, without seeking through all the days and years of his life to understand it, appreciate it, and come to the place where its truth and teachings are the very focus of his living?

The Bible is the norm, the standard, for the doctrines that are to be taught and used in Christian education. How are we to know whether we are teaching the truth? We usually test in terms of Biblical understanding on the premise that God has made himself clear in the Bible, and that if we go to the Bible to find out what he has said we shall be able to interpret for our day what the central doctrines to be used in Christian education are.

We have in the churches, the church schools, and other Christian education agencies a unique responsibility for teaching Bible content. Take qualities like justice, righteousness, truth, and love. These can and must be taught in the schools. They underlie all our culture. Even the newspapers insist upon them. They are the things that Government officials are anxious to see become the very core of our public life. But the schools, the newspapers, and the Government are not going to teach the Bible to the point of Christian commitment. Who, then, is to do it? The central responsibility rests with the home and with the church; primarily with the home, secondarily with the church. The church's major job is not to see that the Bible is taught within its walls; this is its secondary task. Its major job is to see that in every home within its fellowship and community the Bible is taught daily, comprehensively, and competently, so that children, youth, and adults will grow in their grasp of Biblical truth.

THE WORD OF GOD

Allusion has been made several times already in this chapter to the concept of the Word of God. Our best use of the Bible in Christian education depends upon a correct understanding of the Word of God. This is sometimes a badly misunderstood doctrine. It must be dealt with in discussing the Bible and in discussing Jesus Christ.

What is a word? It is a way of getting something across so that it will be understood. I stand before a group and make noises that I have been trained to make. My training in this respect is from childhood on. In a gathering of people who did not understand English the chances are that my noises would mean nothing. My listeners would not be able to make out or understand the words.

The Word of God is God's attempt to get the nature of his being and his will across to us so that we shall understand it. Of course, it is more than the spoken word. As a rule, we regard the Word of God as not so much spoken as written, written in a book. But this again is not by any means the whole concept of the Word. Look again at ordinary words and you see what is involved. To help people to understand something you can show them what it is; you can tell them what it is; and you can make it possible for them constantly to be reminded of it. God uses all these methods: demonstrating, telling, and reminding us of his nature, existence, and truth. He shows us what he is like; here is the Word made flesh, Jesus Christ, pre-existent, existent in history, and eternally existent as the living Christ, the living Lord. He leaves us a written record of what he is like; here is the Bible, the Word in written form. Furthermore, he continually illumines our understanding of what he is like; here is the testimony of the Spirit to the Word within our hearts.

As we read the Bible it may seem like an ordinary book to us. We may go on reading it for years and see only history, drama, epigrams, biography, and the like. But the time will come when reading it we shall realize that through it God is speaking his word to us. This is one form of the testimony of the Spirit to the Word. Unless the Spirit bears witness to the Word in every generation and in every individual life, the Word does not come to life again and it is impossible for us to know, to experience, and to live in the living Christ, the living Lord, the living Word.

The Problem of Correct Interpretation

How may we be as sure as possible that we are reading and studying the Bible so as to interpret it correctly? There are at least three tests that will, I think, stand up in our experience.

Are the contents of the Bible familiar to us? If they are not, then we need be very hesitant indeed as to whether or not we are giving a correct interpretation of the Word.

Are we the kinds of persons who are likely to be able to interpret the Word correctly? In other words, are we as we attempt to interpret the Word possessed of the fruits of the Spirit of God? " By their fruits ye shall know them " (Matt. 7:20). The fruits of the spirit if they are characteristic of our lives are an indication that we are possessed by the Spirit of God. " The fruit of the Spirit is love, joy, peace, long-suffering, gentleness, goodness, faith, meekness, temperance " (Gal. 5:22, 23). One who seriously studies the Scriptures, who is possessed of the Spirit and shows its fruit in his life, is faced with fewer obstacles standing between himself and an understanding of the Word; he is becoming prepared to receive and interpret it correctly.

As we interpret the Word, is the interpretation we give the simplest one that we can discover that does justice to the Word? We see around us attempts to interpret the Word of God that are so difficult, so complicated, so involved, that only a few people can possibly wend their way through the labyrinths that are involved. Certainly if God is speaking his word to us, he does not speak it in riddles. He does not purposely make himself unclear.

WHAT THE BIBLE TEACHES

What does the Bible principally teach? There are four things that cannot be omitted from an understanding of the Bible. First, the Bible teaches how God handled his people until the time of his full revelation in Christ, and it shows how they grew ready for that full revelation. Secondly, it teaches how the Word became flesh and dwelt among us in the person of Jesus Christ. Thirdly, it teaches how God's love overcame the powers of sin, overcame the powers of human nature, and in Christ's death, resurrection, and ascension established firmly the hope of abundant, everlasting life for mankind. Fourthly, it teaches the reality of the Kingdom of God and how that Kingdom is approximated in the Church. The Bible shows what the Church must teach and how it must live if it is to represent its living Lord in each generation.

PRINCIPLES TO GUIDE THE USE OF THE BIBLE IN CHRISTIAN EDUCATION

As Christian educators we need principles that will guide our use of the Bible. Those which follow are drawn from the nature of the faith, the nature and function of the Bible, and the needs of the pupil.

The honest practice of Christian education depends upon the recognition of the threefold nature of the Word as the Word made flesh, the written record, and the Spirit's testimony to the Word in the heart of the believer, and seeks to develop the experience of the Word in each person as the experience that makes clear the meaning of all the rest of life.

The stories and ideas in the Bible are to be taught in accordance with the capacity of the learner to grasp and understand them. This is the principle of grading.

The stories and ideas of the Bible are to be taught in accordance with the learner's need for them and his interest in learning them. This is the principle of readiness.

It is to be recognized that the doctrinal understanding of Biblical truth is primarily for those of mature years and experience, but that such knowledge is not absolutely necessary that one may come to the living Lord. Our chief test for entrance into the fellowship of the Church is the test of discipleship. We do not, except in testing our leaders, use involved doctrinal tests as qualification for membership.

The Christian seeks all possible guidance in Bible study from those who have gone before and have in scholarly fashion sought to solve its problems. He sits at the feet of those who today are seeking correct knowledge of the Word.

The Christian educator looks upon childhood as a period of preparation so far as Biblical understanding is concerned. He seeks to lay solid foundations upon which a mature understanding of the Bible and its message may later be built.

The Christian educator is not satisfied until mature understanding is attained and until the teachings and truth of the Bible are known and experienced.

The Christian educator lives with his Bible that it may become the Word of God to him and that he may become a living epistle testifying to its truth.

The Christian educator as an evangelist seeks primarily to minister to human needs, especially human spiritual need, through the direct application of Biblical truth to the problems of those with whom he deals.

This is something of the scope of our approach in dealing with the Bible. The Bible is the Word of truth to us; through it God speaks to us; it is essentially to us the one indispensable book.

Chapter 7

WHAT THE CHURCH IS FOR

THE MOST PROMISING APPROACH to Christian education is to regard it as nurture within a fellowship, or nurture within a community. The fellowship within which Christian nurture takes place is not limited to what we know as the organized Church. It takes place within the larger community to the extent that the larger community is Christian. It takes place in a very important and significant way in the home, if the home is a Christian fellowship. But this chapter is concerned primarily with the importance of nurture within the fellowship of the organized Church of Jesus Christ.

WHAT IS THE CHURCH?

Americans tend to think of the Church as an organization, an association, or a society. Too often the church is regarded as one among many organizations in the community. It is reasoned that it is good for the community to have churches, but implicit in the reasoning is the assumption that the civil community is the more important unit of society and that the church's function is simply to help that civil unit to be a good community in which to live. This is less than an adequate conception of the nature and function of the church.

In Protestant thought this thing that we know as the church — the building, the organization, or the society — is only an approximation of the Church of Jesus Christ. The true Church includes that cloud of witnesses who have gone before, who surround us even now — the believers, the faithful — those whom God in

Christ has chosen to be his witnesses in the world and his witnesses in eternity. The church that we see is only a reflection of
the true and invisible Church.

The Church visible consists, many Protestants hold, of the
community of the faithful, together with their children. Need-
less to say, it is not identified with any particular denomination,
organization, or institution.

" I believe in . . . the holy Catholic Church." In these words
the Apostles' Creed states the nature of the Church, for the
Church is holy and catholic. It is holy in the sense that it consists of the company of the faithful, the community of believers,
dedicated wholly to the service of God. Being a believer, or one
of the faithful, means that one's whole person is dedicated to the
service and worship of God.

The Church is catholic in the sense that it is always inclusive
of all believers. It is without geographical, racial, or organizational bounds. But it is catholic in another sense; it influences the
whole life of mankind. Our denominations and local churches
are divided and fragmented. But fundamentally we are not un-
related segments. If we are the Church, then we are that united,
visible company of those on earth who believe in the living
Christ.

The Church is the Church of Jesus Christ. It cannot be, if it is
the Church, anything else. Its authority is derived from him; its
life is dedicated to him; it is sustained at every point, to the extent that it is the Church, by his spirit and by his reality. Because
its authority is derived from him, because its life is dedicated to
him, and because it is sustained — of all societies, of all communities, and of all fellowships — by his spirit and by his reality, it is
the body of Christ.

There is another way of putting this matter of the nature of
the Church, not in opposition to anything that has been said already, but to supplement it. When we carry on Christian nurture
within the fellowship of the Christian Church, we are doing it
within the fellowship of love. In the Church, through Christ and
through the spirit of God working in its organization and its

members, the love of God is reflected. Where may we look for the love of God except to Christ? Where may we look for the working out of God's purposes in the world if not to the Church, to those who in dedicated discipleship throughout the world are trying to realize the love of God in Christ and help to reflect it in all of life?

The Church as the fellowship of love also has the responsibility for making love real in the human community. The church is the leaven in the lump of the community; it is the leaven in the lump of the world and the nation. What is the nature of that leaven but the love of God? This is why it is imperative that the Christian Church plan and work for a community, a nation, and a world of love.

The Church, then, in a true sense is this cloud of witnesses around, the community of the faithful together with their children, the holy, catholic Church, the Church of Jesus Christ, and the fellowship of love.

THE CHURCH WE KNOW

Is this the church that we know? Every church that we know has roots. It has its roots, if it is anything like the true Church, in Jesus Christ: in his life, his death, his resurrection, and his ascension. It has its roots in his foundation of the Church as the enduring fellowship of his disciples. Furthermore, each one of our churches has important roots in unique discoveries of the nature of Jesus Christ, his relationship to God, and his revelation of God as the Word.

One of the remarkable things about Protestantism is its richness and its variety. If you maintain that there are no essential differences between the various Churches in your community, you miss the point that true believers throughout the centuries have discovered new things about Jesus Christ and his revelation, have discovered new things about God and his nature, and have been moved in different fashion by the Spirit. Their churches have taken on the characteristics of their particular insights.

The church is a fellowship of members. A member by definition is a part of something. He ceases to be a member if he exists and operates by himself. The church member exists and operates together with other members for purposes that no one of them alone could achieve.

The church has structure. It is organized to do a job. Again, one of the riches of Protestantism is that it has so many different kinds of organization, each one set up to do the specific job that it regards as the most important and most germane to the Christian life and the Christian Church.

WHAT IS THE CHURCH FOR?

The church has function. It exists that men may worship. It exists that men may hear and learn the Word, that they may be stirred and directed by it. It exists that men may assemble in the joy of loving discipleship. It exists that men may together practice the teachings of the gospel in their lives and in the world, and spread throughout the world the light of Christian truth and the warmth of Christian love.

The church is here for worship. It is here that the quality of Christian devotion may be present in the world. It is here that men may come together in public worship. It is here that men may be guided, trained, directed, and supported in private, individual, personal worship. It is here that men may gather around the Table of our Lord and commune together and with him.

The Church is here that the Word may be preached and taught. This is its teaching function. We call our ministers, when we denote one of their chief functions, teachers. The church is here that teaching may be done through preaching, through Christian education, and through other means.

The church is here that the Christian fellowship may be maintained, that it may be instituted with Baptism, that it may be expressed in the life that we live in common, and that it may be expressed in mutual discipline in accordance with the law of Christ.

The church is here that Christians may have social and divine support in their action as witnesses for Christ: witnesses in their vocations, witnesses in the establishment of God's justice in the world, witnesses in the establishment of his righteousness in the world, witnesses that his mercy may be expressed and felt in the world, witnesses that the healing function of the Christian faith may be performed, witnesses that the teaching function of the Christian faith may be performed in the church and beyond its membership, witnesses that evangelism may be maintained and extended, and witnesses that missions may be maintained and made effective throughout all the world.

Some complain that the churches are invading areas of human life that are not their concern. With such a conception of the church as we have outlined, it can hardly be charged that it is usurping functions that rightfully belong to other institutions. In practice, if the church does not perform the functions enumerated in the last four paragraphs it is in danger of ceasing to be the church.

The religious life of America is reported to be much more vital than that of Europe. American observers indicate that this may very well be due to the fact that European churches often have become almost exclusively places of worship, with no closely connected charities, social or recreational activities, or educational activities, thus becoming divorced from the life of the people. A lack of vitality is occasioned by the separation of the Christian Church from the concerns of the people.

What is the Church for? It is the function of the Church to realize the will of God through the spirit of the living Christ in a dedicated society, to nurture the young in that dedicated society, and through it to represent its living Lord in the world.

In such a fellowship, such a community, such a dedicated society Christian nurture may take place. This is the setting for the fulfillment of education for the life in Christ. Within it the development of creative Christian leadership can take place. Thus Christian education is nurture within the fellowship or community of the Church, the fellowship of love and creative discipleship.

Chapter 8

SEEKING AND BELIEVING

SEEKING AND BELIEVING are two essential and complementary aspects of the Christian life. Those who seek are on the way; those who believe have, in a sense, arrived. The process of searching should eventuate in finding. Questions are raised; eventually answers are found.

THE SEARCH FOR TRUTH, BEAUTY, AND GOODNESS

There are churches that make seeking the mark of the Christian life. They ask people when they come into the membership whether it is their determination to seek with them for truth. They are not so much interested in persons' having arrived at certain beliefs; they are more interested in the motivation of the seeker, feeling that if the person is searching — genuinely, sincerely, and with his whole heart — he will find, and that it is better for him to be thus in the mood for search than it is for him to have arrived and closed his mind to further experience and further quest.

One would not want, however, to continue all his life merely in the mood of search; it would be like perpetual spiritual adolescence. But if we do not include ongoing search as a permanent part of the Christian life, we have cut something basic out of our experience. Possibly we have lost the very thing that Christ gave us, that openness to God, to other people, and to new experience that leads us on to new heights of experience and to new heights of assurance.

This is very important, because the world is so large, human knowledge is so complex and involved, and God is so far beyond us in his greatness, his majesty, his will, and his purpose that it is inconceivable that in all of life we could search out and discover even a segment of what in reality he has to offer. Something of a balance is needed between continuous, open, and ready search and the feeling of having arrived at some of the answers, having thus a foundation for life.

Some years ago the youth programs of the Protestant churches were emphasizing what was called " the Christian quest." This is an appropriate thing for young people, for if there is anything that characterizes the spiritual nurture of the adolescent in our culture it is learning the skills of search, and the practice of those skills that he may to an adequate extent find.

The Christian life is often spoken of as man's search for God. The object of the search is God, the reality and the spirit of God. It is also a search for his will, the truth about him, and the truth about all the interrelationships between him and the world, the universe, nature, and society. It is the search for the good life, for which the truth about our relationship with him is normative.

It is the search for righteousness, for God is a righteous God who demands righteousness of his people. We cannot know what righteousness is or how to achieve it unless we search for him, know him, and find from him how it may be known and lived.

There are certain aspects of the search that are too easily neglected. It is all too often thought of as primarily an intellectual search. If you are exploring experience for the purpose of coming to beliefs, you tend to think of the process as one of gaining and refining ideas; almost exclusively is it considered an intellectual process. Make no mistake, the characteristic that differentiates us from other aspects of reality is in the main our ability to use our minds for the purpose of remembering and for the purpose of planning. But there is more to this search than just a search for intellectual belief that is correct and adequate.

The search includes aesthetic search, for we are primarily people of feeling, given to emotion. As religious people we are pri-

marily engaged in an emotional kind of experience, for religion
is primarily a matter of the emotions. We are engaged in an
aesthetic search that, through our feelings and emotions, and
through the integrity that comes through the use of feelings and
emotions in religion, we may express two things adequately and
beautifully: what we find as a result of the search, and the quality
of the search itself.

We seek to create buildings that speak of the search for God
and his reality. We write poetry that often expresses, better than
prose could, the things we feel and think, in their unity. We use
painting; as we stand before the paintings that express the great
emotions of the Christian life we are overwhelmed by the adequacy of the thing that is said on the canvas about the truth of
the Christian life and the reality behind it that is God. We use
various forms of the arts, various aesthetic mediums, to express
the nature of the search and to express the findings of the
search.

Much of modern painting is difficult to understand. Is the
painter in our day perhaps trying to say that it is difficult to find
and interpret clearly the meaning of life, reality, and the universe? When we find his paintings vague and baffling, are we seeing what he is trying to say to us: that it is a hard thing to search
and a difficult thing to find; that the search carried on genuinely
and sincerely does not always eventuate in our finding with clarity and direct understanding? The kind of painting that leaves
us with questions may be an indication of the reality of the
search and the nature of the search in our day.

If we are honest with ourselves, we will admit that for us the
search is to a great extent baffling, the results are often vague and
hard to interpret, and the nature of reality is to a great extent
beyond our understanding and comprehension. Very often it
takes an aesthetic medium to say this. It takes music, painting,
sculpture, or architecture. It is often easier and more effective to
express the nature of the search in these ways than it is to do so
philosophically.

The search involves search for ethical clarity and direction. Of late years we have been made increasingly aware of and sensitive to ethical issues. In emphasizing them we may occasionally have neglected the other aspects of the search, but the ethical aspects of the Christian life are certainly becoming clearer to us.

Here are the three major aspects of our search for God: the search for knowledge of him that is sure — intellectual search; the search for knowledge of him that commends itself to us through our deepest feelings — the aesthetic aspect of the search; and the search for his will — ethical search.

METHODS FOR THE SEARCH

Let us come to grips with the methods that we use in our search for God. There are four that we may use. We all combine them to some extent. Probably the most satisfactory way to search for God and to search for truth is to combine all of them and to use all their resources. The four methods are experience, reason, intuition, and revelation.

How do we search for anything? What is the base of our search for any kind of knowledge or truth? Its base is our experience. Since our birth we have gradually gained, refined, and organized our experience until we know fairly certainly those things upon which we may depend; we have certain basic principles upon which we operate; and we know as Christians that we are thus persons of principle rooted in experience. It is out of experience — our experience with life, with other people, with nature, and with God — that these principles emerge.

Our experience is not only gained; it is refined and organized. How do we deal with our experience so that we know which aspects are true and which are false? How do we know which of its aspects are good and which are evil?

One of the major methods that we use is that of reason. We apply thought to the experience that we have had, so that we know that there are certain kinds of experience that we want to continue and others that we want to do away with.

One of the tools of reason is logic. Logic consists of those rules of thought which in the past have proved themselves as suitable for the refinement and systematization of experience. To think logically is to come to the place where we have some assurance that out of the welter of experience we may be able to arrive at truth.

Protestants as a rule are more pessimistic than others about the ability of man to think his way through to truth by himself. The very reality, power, will, purpose, and presence of God has to be infused into every act of ours, his grace has to operate through us, that our experience and reason may approximate the truth. God must enlighten the understanding of man before man can think clearly and systematically through to what is actually true. If we are to come to ultimate, eternal truth the Protestant principle works most clearly. Ultimate, eternal truth, that it may be known, depends upon the operation of the grace of God in the heart of the disciplined thinker and in the mind of the person of wide experience.

A third method that we use in our search for God is intuition. The word may be confusing, but the meaning is clear when other words are used to explain its function. Insight gives us clues to truth; illumination and creative clarification give us clues to truth. Intuition is insight, illumination, and creative clarification.

Intuition is an important basis even for scientific discovery. The scientist, especially the pioneering scientist who is trying to think through a new and baffling problem, may spend a great deal of time mulling over it. Eventually a solution may dawn on him. Call it intuition, insight, illumination, creative clarification, what you will. He subjects it to experiment. Perhaps it works, perhaps not. If it works, he has it. If not, then he goes back to it to work further. But from time to time intuition will give him direction; clarification and insight come.

We know that where we could never arrive at truth by taking things step by step in systematic order, through reason, we can and do arrive at it through intuition. This is why intuition is one of the methods of our search.

The fourth method is revelation. Revelation is not properly

spoken of as a method that we use, for revelation is God's initiative. Revelation is the process by which God makes himself, his purposes, his will, and his plan clear to us. From our point of view the process is one of devout and careful understanding of revelation, learning what it is that God is trying to reveal to us. In order to understand the truth that God is trying to reveal to us we have to use all the powers of experience, reason, and intuition.

Another way of expressing these methods is in terms of the disciplines that are involved in their use. We search for truth through science; while science has its limitations, nevertheless it gives us the kind of truth that we need in the areas in which it is legitimately used. We use the method of philosophy, combining intuition, experience, and reason, but using primarily the processes of reason. We use the method of religion. In religion all four of the processes are involved, for while religion primarily involves revelation, it involves the appropriation, the grasping of that revelation through experience, through reason, and through intuition.

GOD'S SEARCH FOR MAN

The Christian discovers in the process of search a truth he possibly has not foreseen: that the Christian life is not properly man's search for God at all. The Christian life is more properly God's search for man. The objects of the search — truth, righteousness, and the good life — become clearer when we realize that it is God who is searching for us.

Why is man sought by God? Man is sought by God because man is created in his image, because through sin that image is distorted, and because God knows that it can be restored. It is his will that it be restored in all its clarity and beauty through the redemption and salvation that he has made possible. Unless God makes the restitution of his image in man possible, it cannot be restored.

How has God searched for man? He has searched for man in history. It is in the events of man's life that God has sought him.

It is as a creature that man has been sought. In the Bible the picture is often given of God's coming in person, as it were, to seek man.

The Jewish people thought of God as operating in their history and in the history of the world. Jonah, for instance, discovered that he could not get away from the working of God in history. He could not avoid the will of God by leaving his country. He discovered that God had jurisdiction over the whole world and over all of history.

God has sought us in history through Jesus Christ who is his revelation in history. God has sought us in history through his Word. It is because through Christ and the Word he has sought us that we speak of Jesus Christ as the Word made flesh and speak of the living Christ as the living Word.

God seeks us, as it were, in person. He abides with us; he leads us; he is never absent from us. God is searching now for man. In present events he is confronting man in this day, in this place. He confronts man redemptively as man encounters him in Christ.

It has been put clearly and poignantly in these lines from a well-known hymn:

> "I sought the Lord, and afterward I knew
>   He moved my soul to seek Him, seeking me;
> It was not I that found, O Saviour true;
>   No, I was found of Thee.
>
> "Thou didst reach forth Thy hand and mine enfold;
>   I walked and sank not on the storm-vexed sea;
> 'Twas not so much that I on Thee took hold
>   As Thou, dear Lord, on me.
>
> "I find, I walk, I love, but O the whole
>   Of love is but my answer, Lord, to Thee
> For Thou wert long beforehand with my soul;
>   Always Thou lovedst me"
>
>   (Anonymous).

The initiative of God is the heart of the Christian faith, the key to the Christian life. The search is not so much our search.

Our search is a search that God himself has initiated in his
search for our redemption.

The result of God's search for man is man's voluntary obedience to him, which in turn is freedom, the human freedom in
Christ that makes possible the righteousness that man cannot establish for himself without God's initiative in his redemption.

THE MEANING AND INTEGRITY OF BELIEF

One of the results of the search is firm belief. What is belief?
We properly think of it in terms of beliefs about ultimate truth.
We talk of belief in God, in the Word of God, in matters of uni-
versal import.

But we do not always use the term in this fashion. We use it
in at least three other ways. We talk of belief as truth to be as-
sented to but not necessarily used. We use it in the sense of the
truth that is arrived at through the generalization of our experience. We use it also in the sense of truth upon which action may
be based.

In these three uses of *belief,* we confront a continuing problem
of the Christian life. It is that of matching belief and practice,
the problem of Christian integrity. At the point where we believe that which we do not do, where we arrive at answers that
we do not put into practice, our problem is lack of integrity, disparity between belief and practice.

There are ways, however, in which this disparity may be reduced, and integrity made more possible. We can straighten out
in practice personal attitudes that do not match our beliefs. The
place to check whether personal attitudes at work match our beliefs is in practical life experiences.

We can deal with specific problems. The problems that we
meet personally in the family, business, church, community, and
our larger relationships are the proving grounds of our basic beliefs. If we deal with them specifically one by one, we may be able
to handle them. Problems can be taken step by step. Advance
toward integrity that can be planned for and carried through is

more valuable than the vague ideal that is left without implementation.

We can take effective local action. One place to deal with large national and international issues is on the level of the local community or church. Here the skills may be developed that mean effectiveness in the larger field.

In dealing with problems we must continue to be concerned with human relations. Differences of opinion will develop, but the opposition is made up of persons of intrinsic worth, children of God, who are to be treated as such.

We can develop awareness of the support that God gives to righteousness by being what he is, awareness of what might be called " the cosmic guarantee." Impetus is given to the goals implied in our basic beliefs if they may be sincerely interpreted as the will of God.

We can articulate our beliefs at appropriate times. When the time comes, the Christian will say clearly, " This I believe," or, " Here I stand."

We can seek reorientation in prayer. Beliefs and practices both change and are reinterpreted as God's will becomes clearer through creative fellowship with him.

Chapter 9

TO LIVE IS CHRIST

ONE OF THE MOST mystifying of all the questions that occur to the human mind is the question of the existence and nature of God. Who is God? Where is he? What is he like? How do we come to know him? What does he want with man?

We are very likely to put at least two of the questions more personally. How may I come to know him? What does he want with me? What does he want with the child I seek to lead, or the youth, or the adult?

The search for God, the ceaseless quest to answer the question of his existence and nature and the question of his relationships to us, starts very early. Until we reach adolescence, perhaps late adolescence or even maturity, our knowledge of God grows and changes very rapidly. In our first relationships with our environment — with our parents, our friends, our teachers, and all the rest — we are exploring our world and discovering the existence and nature of the God who undergirds, creates, and wills that world.

Have we become so callous to the reality of God that we do not remember that God in Christ is real in the world, in the environment and in the life of even the little child? Perhaps our world has become so secularized that we do not realize that God is the reality of realities. Even though the child may not put it into adequate words, or know God as he will know him in maturity, yet God sustains a Father's relationship to him.

LIFE'S FUNDAMENTAL QUESTIONS

Our religious development may be symbolized by the asking and answering of four questions. They may be phrased in complicated ways by philosophers, but I am indebted to the late Ruth D. Perry, who for many years directed the Riverside Church Nursery School, for her simple and direct statement of them: Who am I? Who are you? Where do I live? Why do I live?

Who am I? Every glance, every reaching out of the hands, every step that is taken, every hesitation, every acceptance of the life around me, every determination of personal role: these are the raising and answering of the question, Who am I?

Who are you — my father, my mother, my children, my friends and associates? Who are you really? And how are you and your purposes related to me?

Where do I live? This universe of mine — at first it is just the crib; then it is the home, the neighborhood, the heavens, the world, and the universe beyond the world. This universe of mine — what is it? Who am I in relation to it? When I ask the question, even if I ask it without words, I am trying to find out who God is, because I am living in the universe that is God's.

Why do I live? The question is not only the crux of the personal approach to the matter; it is the culmination of the search that involves the other three. It is not likely to be voiced until the child is perhaps six years old. It is when his experience has broadened beyond the family and the immediate neighborhood that the problem of the meaning and destiny of his life becomes urgent.

THE WORLD'S ANSWERS

There are a variety of answers that the world gives to the question of who God is, where he is, what he is like, how he is known, and what he asks of man.

There is the naturalistic answer. The naturalistic view is that God is nature and nature is God. There is no God above or beyond the natural order. With the help of scientific methods we discover the laws by which nature operates, and it is as if we had discovered the laws of God. Naturalism is not a philosophy that takes much stock in prayer and worship. It does not as a rule look kindly upon the traditions of religion. It is, as a matter of fact, very often the avowed foe of the Christian faith and the Christian idea of God. Yet this philosophy is current and influential in our day in this nation.

Humanism is a warmer point of view than naturalism, for it looks into the heart of the human being for those values and truths that can really direct and make life worth-while. It holds that the human mind and heart are the keys to life's meaning. In the human mind and heart and in human society are to be found the clues to the understanding of the good life. But in this philosophy anything that we call God is simply the accumulation of our human ideas of the good and the valuable. Anything that we call God is simply the highest that human beings have been able to conceive; there is no objectively real personal God to match these high ideas.

Secularism is the answer of many in our day to the question of the nature and reality of God. Secularism is the organization of life as if there were certain aspects of life with which God had no concern. To the secularist religion has a legitimate place in life. When it comes to the issues of God, religious ideas, the church, and the like, religion has its place. But there are aspects of life that have no connection with or relevance to religion. Here the secularist seeks other laws and other guidance. To him education, commerce, international affairs, and other crucial human concerns operate by their own laws, and the laws and the guidance of religion are irrelevant. When it comes to these, the secularist will often allow a chaplain but not a prophet.

Often, although we have not avowedly accepted secularism, we have acted as if its point of view were true. We in Christian education know that the children who come to us in the church are often deeply convinced that what is said and done there does not apply in certain other areas of their lives. This is the essence of secularism. Here life is clearly divided into two or more segments.

In one segment religion and religious ideas count; in the others they do not. This does not deny the reality of God; it simply puts him in another room.

There is also that great cloud that hangs over us, and over so much of the world — the philosophy of totalitarianism. For totalitarianism the consummate reality is not God but Caesar. The real decisions and power are in the hands of the State. Newspapers, radio, television, our schools, and even our churches lie under the potential blight of totalitarianism, and here again the influence upon us is great.

THE CHRISTIAN ANSWER

Naturalism, humanism, secularism, totalitarianism — what of the Christian view? The Christian answer is that God reveals himself to us in Jesus Christ, who is the very Word of God spoken to us. God is the will, purpose, and reality creating and undergirding all of life and the universe — all of society, national life, community life, our churches, ourselves, and even nature itself. God is this reality: creative, undergirding, willing, purposing, and guiding.

This God would not keep himself hidden from his people. It is impossible to conceive of a God of righteousness, truth, and love choosing to remain unknown. No, he has revealed himself to us; he has shown himself to us in Christ. He has spoken his Word and communicated to us of his nature in Christ. In Christ is righteousness, truth, and love: God's righteousness, God's truth, and God's love.

This is the God who surrounds the life of the little child, who surrounds and guides the life of youth, and who guides and leads and informs the life of maturity. The life in Christ is the goal of Christian education because Christ is the revelation of God to man, and because in the living Christ men may become sons of God.

It is not simply, however, that God reveals himself to man. Such a revelation could be just an arbitrary movement on God's part to demonstrate himself. No, he reaches out in the living

Christ to redeem man, that in Christ we may become sons and
daughters of his. He not only shows himself, but redeems mankind. This is the reality of his love.

The child, the youth, or the adult who starts out to search for
God finds that the Christian answer is that he is sought of God.
This is the personal relevance of the doctrines of relevation and
redemption. For him who is sought of God, to live is Christ.

Who was Christ? What did he do? Who is he? The *Brief Statement of the Reformed Faith* (adopted in 1902 by the Presbyterian Church in the U.S.A.) sums up what Christ was, what he
did, and what he is:

> " We believe in and confess the Lord Jesus Christ, the only Medi-
> ator between God and man, who, being the Eternal Son of God,
> for us men and for our salvation became truly man, being con-
> ceived by the Holy Ghost and born of the Virgin Mary, without
> sin; unto us He has revealed the Father, by His Word and Spirit
> making known the perfect will of God; for us He fulfilled all
> righteousness and satisfied eternal justice, offering Himself a per-
> fect sacrifice upon the cross to take away the sin of the world;
> for us He rose from the dead and ascended into heaven, where
> He ever intercedes for us; in our hearts, joined to Him by faith,
> He abides forever as the indwelling Christ; over us, and over all
> for us, He rules: wherefore, unto Him we render love, obedience,
> and adoration as our Prophet, Priest, and King forever."

Any education that is Christian is dependent upon an understanding of him and seeks a growing experience of him.

Who was Christ? From the beginning those who knew him
thought of Jesus as different from other people — not remote or
distant, but the kind of person who won the hearts of men, who
had access to a source of power and winsomeness beyond any they
had reckoned with before. It is from Paul that much of the idea
of who Christ was is drawn. By the time he wrote his letters defining Christian faith and practice, the Church had crystallized
and articulated its experience with Jesus Christ into a point of
view that it could communicate convincingly to others. To him,
Christ was the Messiah, yet he was more than some prevailing no-

tions of the Messiah since he spoke not so much to a nation as to each individual and to the whole world.

Paul tells us clearly who Christ was when he says: " Let this mind be in you, which was also in Christ Jesus: who, being in the form of God, thought it not robbery to be equal with God: but made himself of no reputation, and took upon him the form of a servant, and was made in the likeness of men: and being found in fashion as a man, he humbled himself, and became obedient unto death, even the death of the cross. Wherefore God also hath highly exalted him, and given him a name which is above every name: that at the name of Jesus every knee should bow, of things in heaven, and things in earth, and things under the earth; and that every tongue should confess that Jesus Christ is Lord, to the glory of God the Father " (Phil. 2: 5–11).

This, then, was not an isolated instance of a human life lived two thousand years ago in a distant province of the Roman Empire. This was the occasion on which Almighty God showed us what he was by becoming one of us.

What Christ was begins to dawn on the youth when he is leaving childhood behind. It is then that, in his search for the meaning of life, he may find for himself that through Jesus Christ God reaches out to him and offers him life that is abundant and eternal.

What did Christ do? He was born; he grew; he was baptized; he was tempted; he preached; he taught; he healed; he prayed; he gathered disciples; he set his face steadfastly to go to Jerusalem; he ate with his disciples; he was crucified; he rose from the dead; he ascended.

The story needs to be told, incident by incident, over and over again, lovingly and meditatively, that we may become filled with the knowledge of the life that he led and the truth that he taught.

It is in childhood that we begin to tell the story; it is in youth that its meaning begins to come clear to us and our burning hearts begin to acknowledge him. He grows on us; every day that we seek to know more of him and to learn more perfectly to do his will we gain some ground in the life he asks us to lead.

Who is Christ? " Lo, I am with you alway, even unto the end of the world " (Matt. 28: 20) . He is for us the living Christ, the indwelling Christ. Paul again says it for us: " I am crucified with Christ: nevertheless I live; yet not I, but Christ liveth in me: and the life which I now live in the flesh I live by the faith of the Son of God, who loved me, and gave himself for me " (Gal. 2: 20) . What is the greatest thing in the world? What is the Christian's most precious possession? It is the sense of the living, indwelling Christ. It is thus that we come close to God; it is thus that we may be found of his spirit.

What of the Christ of maturity? When childhood's questionings and wonderings have been satisfied, when youth's perplexities and doubts have been overcome, we have still to grow in grace. It is then, when we are mature, that we may grow in the knowledge and love of God through the living Christ.

What of this for Christian education? The answer is clear: the teacher, knowing Christ himself and seeking by his help to grow in full Christian living, helps the child to know what Christ did, helps the youth to know who Christ was and to live in him, and helps the grown person to increase ever in the spiritual life in him.

Christian education includes many things; it teaches many things; there is nothing in life or the universe that it cannot deal with. Yet all that is taught, and all that is dealt with, is in order that Christ may be made manifest and that man may find himself in him.

Part Three

THE TRANSFORMATION OF PERSONALITY

Chapter 10

WHAT PERSONALITY IS

How does the Christian life come into being? How does Christian nurture take place in the individual? Its organization in the home, the church, and the community depends upon the conception of its process in basic terms.

If we maintain that Christian education is the transformation and reconstruction of personality toward the life in Christ, some fundamental questions about personality are indicated. We must ask what personality is, how it develops, and how it may become Christian.

What Is a Person?

What is personality? In order to come at the question in the simplest terms possible, let us begin by asking what makes a person different from a thing. The distinction must be made between personhood and thinghood if we are to get at the nature of personality. Both things and persons have substance and structure. We note also that persons move and that some things move. Things, however, seem to move in terms of mechanical laws, while persons seem to respond both to mechanical laws and to other more subtle influences. Here reality is interpreted in terms of substance, structure, movement, and mechanism. Things and persons both function at this level, but persons transcend it.

Note, then, the reality of organism. An organism is a living being that acts and reacts as a whole. Each part of an organism influences all its other parts. Organisms may take the form of living beings on land or in the sea. An organism may be infinitesimally

small or exceedingly large. But its basic characteristic is that it
has some kind of essential unity within itself that leads us to call
it an individual being. With this interdependence of parts within
an organism and their taking on reality and life in terms of the
relationship to their other parts we have the beginnings of feelings and emotion.

But a person is more than a thing or an organism. There is a
tendency to reduce human life and personality to the levels of
thinghood or organism in the attempt at explanation. Seeing the
relationships and similarities between human life and mechanism
and organism, men are led to wonder at them and to be awed and
amazed by them. This sometimes leads them mistakenly to associate human life exclusively with mechanism or organism and to
seek the explanation of human life, its movements, and its integrity in terms of these categories that are actually inadequate to
explain it.

The most obvious thing that distinguishes a person from a
thing or an organism is, as has been pointed out before, his ability to remember yesterday and to plan for tomorrow. He is able
to see today in a perspective that is impossible to a thing and to
lower orders and forms of life. This means of course that persons
pre-eminently have minds. Their minds are interdependent with
their feelings and emotions, but nevertheless the mind can directly affect the organism and guide and direct it. A person having a mind can think; he can reason; he can deal with and analyze problems. In a word, he can guide the process of his life.

Self-consciousness is involved. Other creatures are not self-con-
scious. They do not have the quality of self that human beings
have and are not conscious of self in the way that characterizes
human beings. One of the marks of human life at the level of
self-consciousness is man's ability to see himself as if from the outside. He can act and inspect that action at the same time. Other
creatures cannot. They do not look objectively at what is happening to them.

We can, as it were, stand outside ourselves and look at ourselves. We might think about the word " ourselves " in this case

as two words. We can stand outside our selves and look at our selves. Therefore we are able to some degree objectively to investigate what we are, to look at our motivations and behavior, the total impact of our lives, and to develop direction.

Personality is characterized by planning and purposing. Other organisms are goal-seeking, but they cannot organize anything like the total planning personality — mind, emotions, and will — to seek their goals.

Because persons have minds they develop purposes. Human motives as contrasted with the motives of the lower forms of life are such as may be consciously recognized and consciously organized and carried into action. Thus the mind is brought to bear upon the motive. The mind and spirit interpret the motive, see it in relationship to other possible motives, and organize them until we have a unity that is not just a physical unity but a psychophysical organism.

The individual, the person, is characterized by seeking and finding direction in life. To the extent that he is a person he will thus seek direction and will not be satisfied until he finds it.

The principle involved is the principle of organism, but with a plus. It is the principle of human unity or focus upon a goal that may actually be consciously selected, toward which the individual may direct all his energy, thought, and action.

Here, then, is some clue to personality. It is what distinguishes us from things and from other organisms, and involves such qualities as memory, self-consciousness, and organizing purpose.

THE IMAGE OF GOD

Discussing personality in these terms, we approach a point where it may be seen that because personality is more than mechanism and more than organism some other category is needed to make clear its nature. The Christian faith teaches that man is created in the image of God. Personality cannot be fully understood except as it is seen in relation both to the earth from which it emerges and to God its creator. We think of the purposes of man and see that they can be related to the purposes of God.

Furthermore, we sense that man is not his best self, his highest self, outside this relationship. Personality does not reach its highest achievements unless man is seen as discovering and doing the will of God. This is the psalmist's vision:

> " When I consider thy heavens, the work of thy fingers,
> The moon and the stars, which thou hast ordained;
> What is man, that thou art mindful of him?
> And the son of man, that thou visitest him?
> For thou hast made him a little lower than the angels,
> And hast crowned him with glory and honor.
> Thou madest him to have dominion over the works of thy hands;
> Thou hast put all things under his feet:
> All sheep and oxen,
> Yea, and the beasts of the field;
> The fowl of the air, and the fish of the sea,
> And whatsoever passeth through the paths of the seas"
>
> (Ps. 8:3–8) .

Man is thus seen as a person in the image of God. He is seen as of the earth, living as a creature on the earth, and yet in a special relationship because he, among all creatures, is created in God's image.

SIN AND FREEDOM

It is not enough to say that man is created in the image of God. It is not enough to say that personality is more than mechanism and more than organism. As we contemplate the personalities of individuals that we know and have heard of, we recognize the fact that it is not an adequate description of personality to indicate that man has reached a point where he is engaged in what might be called a divine-human kinship.

The clue to our difficulty at this point will be found in the reality and nature of freedom. One of the characteristics of personality is freedom. Persons can think; they can make up their minds; they can act on their choices; they can make mistakes. If persons were not free, they would not be in the image of God, for God is free and sovereign will. If men were not free, they would be reduced to things or to organisms.

The highest achievements of personality come about because of freedom. Since we are free we can be creative; we can discover and express things that other creatures cannot. We can experience reality and our environment in ways in which no other creature can possibly experience that which is outside himself. We can develop concepts of meaning, interpretations of ourselves and our environment, that no other creature can, and thus creatively we direct and interpret our existence.

But sin comes because of freedom, and sin is an obvious reality in human life. It is clear that personality as it exists does not reflect the image of God without distortion. Persons are given to wickedness, thoughtlessness, carelessness, indifference, laziness, and the like. These traits obscure and blot out God's image in man. Freedom implies the ability to make mistakes, to turn to evil, even to reject God and to refuse to do his will. It implies the ability to sin. Because human beings are created in the image of God and yet are human beings, they are prone to fall into the ways of sin in the very working out of their God-given freedom.

But this is not the whole story of freedom, for it also involves the ability to respond to God with loving and creative obedience. It is because of the necessity for this response that we feel that God has given freedom to man. God is willing to run the risk that the children he loves and cares for may fall into error, make mistakes, and fall into sin in order that they may have the quality within them that will allow them also to respond to him, to come to him, and to receive from him the care, the love, and the guidance that he can give. If man were forced to come to God, the response could not be satisfactory to him. The kind of follower God wants is the follower who comes to him freely out of a full and complete love.

If freedom leads us creatively to interpret ourselves and our environment, we can interpret that environment and its relation to ourselves realistically and theistically. We can say that the outstanding fact and reality in our environment is God. There is no other fact, no other reality, so important and so determinative of our lives and our destinies, of the whole course of our existence, as God himself. In the subordination of our existence to that of God a realistic perspective has come into our situation.

On the other hand, because we are free we can make the mistake that is sin, saying, " I am the master of my fate: I am the captain of my soul." Sin is most characteristically the proneness to this egocentricity. It is when we set ourselves up in place of God that we see ourselves in completely false perspective. To think that we are in charge, that we are the center of the universe, leads us to all kinds of distorted interpretations and distorted behavior. It eventuates in the creation of evil because its separation of the soul from God could eventuate in nothing else.

We are therefore free to see ourselves in realistic perspective, theistic perspective; but we are also free to see ourselves in egocentric perspective. Human freedom can lead in either direction.

RESPONSIBILITY

A further condition that sheds light on personality is responsibility. We know when we see ourselves in proper perspective that human life and the natural world are characterized by interdependence. We depend upon the natural world and upon other persons; other persons depend upon us. There is a mutuality about the whole process of human development. On the human plane responsibility becomes an essential. Responsibility in the human realm is response to the demands and needs of others. It is the ability, in a somewhat larger sense, to respond in appropriate fashion to the natural order and the demands and needs of society. This ability is a way by which we find and obey the law of God.

One cannot say with exactness that God and man are interdependent, or that God and nature are interdependent, because God and man, and God and nature, are in a creator-creature relationship. The relationship is one of dependence. Nature and humanity are dependent upon their Creator. But again an interpretation of the area of responsibility is involved. Responsibility is ability to respond adequately to the demands of God and the opportunities that he sets in our way. Therefore it is an appropriate response to God, as well as to nature and human life.

It is quite obvious that personality cannot be fulfilled in its richness until it becomes really personal in character through the response to God of dependence and the response to nature and to man of interdependence. But it is significant that the only creatures capable of such response are persons.

UNIQUENESS IN PERSONALITY

Personality also has uniqueness. Each person is an individual, differing from every other individual. The individuality of human experience — the kind of experience that an individual has, and his response through that experience to the world around him, to the society around him, and to God — will in each case vary. It is thus that each personality will come to be to some extent unique.

Each individual has a somewhat unique heredity; each responds in somewhat different fashion to the environment. Indeed, the environment itself varies for each because of the selective nature of experience and attention. The developing self becomes of crucial importance. The self, defined as the individual as known to the individual, provides a polarity for experience that guarantees uniqueness.

Each individual's consciousness is unique in perception, imagery, feeling, thought, creativity, purpose, and plan. Each individual struggles with his own conflicts, tensions, and problems. He struggles with aspects of himself, unconscious dynamics, of which he is not aware.

Each individual comes to his own integrity, his own personal unity, wholeness, and focus. He has his own unique membership character. As a member of communities, guided, molded, structured, and inhibited by the lives of others, as a reflection of a developmental history in a specific cultural whole, he yet by virtue of this very interaction becomes himself, unique and individual.

THE QUALITIES OF PERSONALITY

Here we have the basic qualities that go into the making of personality. Personality involves a relationship between the individual and God that is of a special nature, in which he can if he will respond to God as a person, partake of the nature of the divine within his own life, and thus know and do the will of God. Personality is free and responsible; the response that the individual makes to God may be the free, loving response of creative obedience. Personality is unique; each individual is different; he responds differently; his hopes, his aspirations, his ambitions, his achievements are different from those of other persons.

Personality is the characteristic of individuals as they respond with freedom to the opportunities and demands of nature, man, and God. What it may become is the restored image of God, taking on in each case the distinctive form that is fitting to the individual's experience.

This interpretation of personality pictures man in an unusual and unique situation so far as his relation to God and to creation is concerned. Persons are different from things and other creatures, yet the characteristics that make persons different are exactly those that link them to God. When persons are restored to the image of God, they have more of an affinity to God than they have to things and to other creatures.

It is at this point that a transformation takes place in which we find the home of our spirits more truly with God than with the earth or the society out of which we came. This is the most significant thing about personality: that there is in the creation of personality a re-creation of the image of God and thus a breaking of the shackles that have bound the individual to the earth. The reality of personality is personal encounter with the divine.

Chapter 11

HOW PERSONALITY DEVELOPS

THERE ARE THREE FACTORS in the development of personality. They are always found in dynamic relationship to one another.

HEREDITY, ENVIRONMENT, AND THE DEVELOPING SELF

Heredity involves the passing on of traits of various kinds from parents to children through the germ cells of the parents. These are the germ cells that combine to make the new organism. These germ cells, called the genes, determine that the child, provided he has a fairly normal environment, will develop particular traits similar to those of the family from which he comes. They operate clearly in the various species. Because of heredity you may determine on inspection the species of which a particular organism is a part.

If the parents are of certain types, if their bodies contain genes of certain kinds, then there are certain hereditary traits of the parents that are likely to be perfectly obvious in their offspring. In terms of the Mendelian laws a certain amount of prediction may be made as to when traits are going to show up in various generations.

Allport makes the point that so far as personality is concerned two fundamental types of adjustment in infancy, which tend to persist throughout life, are products of inheritance: the intensity and frequency of the infant's spontaneous activity (*motility*) and his emotional expression (*temperament*) (Gordon W. Allport, *Personality, a Psychological Interpretation,* p. 129. Henry Holt & Company, Inc., 1937).

The environment consists of that group of factors that surround the organism and are potentially capable of influencing it. In Christian education we use a very large concept of the environment. Psychology usually limits it to the physical and social world around the individual. In general it is bounded by those particular physical and social influences which are brought to bear directly upon him. In Christian education we consider that the most real aspect of the individual's environment is the existence of God. God, therefore, rather than the physical world or society, becomes the determining, definitive reality in the individual's environment.

However, this might lead to distortion. We proceed to say that for purposes of organizing and carrying through a Christian education program, we consider that the individual's environment consists of the divine, the human, and the natural. Thus God, society, and nature define the larger conception of the environment.

The developing self is the third factor in the development of personality. The self is the individual as known to the individual. To put it a little more personally, the self is " I " as I know myself. The self is a rather subjective thing, but it is the most immediate thing that any of us knows. Descartes, when he had finished doubting everything, found that there was one thing that he could not doubt. That was that he thought. He came to the conclusion that the one firm foundation for philosophical thinking was, " I think, therefore, I am." The basis for existence was his knowledge of the fact that he was a thinking being. In his view, if you really get down to bedrock on what you know, about all that you can know on the basis of any human experience or human proof is the existence of the self.

Theologically, the developing self is based originally upon the image of God. It partakes, however, of the sinful nature of the free creature. The developing self has the potential of becoming again the image of God if God reaches down and guides and controls its development toward himself.

It is the developing self that purposes. It is the developing self that plans. It is the developing self that uses the heredity and the environment, its " givens," in terms of its goals, what it wishes to become, and what it purposes to become. An argument that tries to make heredity the important factor, or environment, and leaves out the factor of what I am myself, what I purpose to become, what I plan to become, and what my aims, goals, and objectives are, is less than adequate.

Elements Involved in the Development of the Self

There are elements basic to the development of the self. It does not develop without them. They include heredity and environment, but a revised and expanded listing will make the process and its elements clearer. Here, then, are some of the important elements in the making of personality:

Biological dispositions. The self is founded upon the coming into existence of certain definite biological dispositions, including the factor of temperament.

The interaction of the individual constitution with a specific environment. This interaction may range all the way from rudimentary curiosity on the part of the individual with regard to his environment, to the reordering of the environment that it may become the setting for the fulfillment of his highest purposes. Mention of these two poles does not minimize the importance of all the gradations between them.

Consciousness. Consciousness includes perception, the process of looking at or sensing that which is outside ourselves and interpreting it for ourselves. Perception and imagery are the creation of symbols that represent what is outside of ourselves, primarily in order that we may be able to remember and use things that we have sensed or experienced. Consciousness includes feeling. It includes thought, which is the systematization or the ordering of the images that are basic to experience. Consciousness includes creativity; it includes purpose; it includes plan.

Unconscious dynamics. Unconscious dynamics sometimes involve a struggle with what might be called the " not-self." There is a great deal that must be contended with in one's own life that is not recognized or avowed. You wonder where a sudden thought came from, or a sudden desire. You wonder why a certain purpose occurred to you. " I am not myself," you say. " This is not like me." Why did you do, think, or say what you did? Unconscious dynamics are operating, and what you would not consciously avow you are and do. Part of the process of dealing with unconscious dynamics is the struggle with that which is less than yourself, less than personal, and with tendencies of which the self is not aware.

Conflict, tension, problem. Personal growth does not take place except where conflict, tension, and problem are present. This is easy to see when it is recognized that every new experience tends, to some degree, to upset the old personal balance and to change the person. Each new experience that comes along has to be grappled with. You have to deal with it, become different, grow, and develop in order to handle the situation that has presented itself. This may seem very negative, yet when conflict, tension, and problem cease the individual is dead. Death, from a purely human point of view, is the cessation of these elements. When conflict ceases, thinking stops. When tension ceases, motivation stops. When problems are no longer present, personality does not develop. In education we inject ourselves purposely into problem situations which we hope will develop us into more adequate persons than we were before.

Integration. Integration balances the matter of conflict, tension, and problem. If conflict persists, if tension is not relieved, if problems are not solved, nothing happens by way of development. Rather, disintegration takes place. But if conflict is resolved, if tensions are released, if problems are solved, integration takes place. Integration in personality means unity, wholeness, focus, and in a sense direction.

Membership character. Here we return to the relation between the developing self and the environment. Each individual to exist has to be a member of a community. Take the community, other people, away from the newborn child, and he cannot live. Human life cannot be supported ultimately aside from community life. Each individual is guided, inhibited, molded, instructed, structured, and nurtured by the life of the community. Each personality is a reflection of a developmental history within a specific cultural whole.

THE ORGANIZATION OF EXPERIENCE

There has developed of late years a larger concept of how we become what we are through experience. Personality develops as experience is gained, refined, and organized.

What is experience? Experience occurs when relationships within one's self, or between one's self and the environment, are used consciously or unconsciously, primarily consciously, to gain a foothold in existence, to interpret it, or to direct its course.

Only persons, in the last analysis, have experience. Types of experience and their use define the individual personality. If you want a definition of a particular individual, find out what kinds or types of experience he has, or has had, and how he has used them.

We gain experience through an expanding apprehension of the reality around us. We look farther and farther out. We get better acquainted with things outside ourselves. We go traveling, inspect things, study, and in the process come to grasp surrounding reality. We have an urge to experience that which is beyond what we have already experienced. When we reach it, we are urged on even farther. Thus we become more experienced.

We gain experience through satisfying the urge to explore and through satisfying our curiosity. Curiosity and the urge to explore are the foundations of education. So long as they are operative, motivation is not lacking.

But the experience we gain is likely to be gross in character. It has to be refined. What is the process of the refinement of experience? You are refining experience when you are responding to motives. Which of the motives that are present at any particular moment are you responding to? Depending on which you respond to, you are refining experience in their direction.

Another of the ways in which we refine experience is through remembering and forgetting. We remember those experiences that we want to remember, want to repeat, and want to keep fresh. We forget those experiences that are relatively meaningless, and make an effort to forget those that we do not want to remember or that we wish had not happened to us. Sometimes we have so refined our experience that there are stimuli that are actually inhibited from entering consciousness.

We refine experience further through defining our purposes. When we have done this, they can help us to select the kinds of experiences in which we will or will not engage. Experience is refined by determining a course of action, a direction, and adhering to it.

How do we organize experience? There is actually an alternation between gaining new experience and organizing it into wholes or unities for personal use. The organization of experience thus includes interpretation and selection of experience, and its systematization into wholes or unities that will be useful to us. We need conflict, tension, and problems in order to make us grow, but development also depends upon their resolution into meanings through which balance and harmony may be achieved. Thus we are continually alternating between gaining new experience, which throws us off balance, and integrating and organizing that experience, leading to the achievement of balance and harmony once more.

The levels of organization of personality have been listed by Allport (*op cit.,* pp. 139, 140). The most primitive level at which there is any learned experience is the *conditioned reflex.* The reflex is inherited. When it is conditioned, learning is taking place in a rudimentary sense. The next level is that of *habit*; habits are accumulations of conditioned reflexes. *Traits* are the further organization of clusters of habits. A trait brings a whole group of habits into focus. The step beyond the trait is the *self,* in terms of which traits are organized within dominant purposes. Finally, the *personality* itself, which is the highest level of organization, comes into being where a dominant purpose or an integration of dominant purposes is so established that it tends to organize the whole system of selves, traits, habits, and conditioned reflexes, and to give balance, harmony, unity, and integration to the whole process.

Organization for meaning is one of the keys to the process. Intellectual functioning in the personality is the organization of experience to achieve meaning, without which personality cannot exist.

In Christian education the culmination of the organization of experience is decision, devotion, and commitment. Sometimes experience becomes suddenly organized in personality; that which has been disintegrated and diffuse before becomes systematized, structured, balanced, and harmonious. This, in a psychological sense, is the reality of conversion.

How does the development of this process of gaining, refining, and organizing experience take place customarily in the individual? The period of childhood is primarily characterized by exploration, the gaining of experience. Adolescence is likely to be characterized by the urgent search for the self, the search for direction, and the definition of one's role. In adolescence certain problems that society poses for the transition between childhood and adulthood have to be solved. To solve them one has to come in the long run to some satisfactory philosophy of life. In maturity there is the gradual and creative building of experience upon the foundations laid in childhood and in youth. Maturity is as a rule the period in life when one makes his major contributions. It is characterized experiencewise by the alternation between struggle to attain and the enjoyment of achievement. Mature worship, prayer, and meditation very often express this alternation best. Balanced and creative living upon a rich background of experience is the sign of maturity.

Personality develops, then, an essential unity and integrity. It is basically individual, not abstract but very concrete. It is a continuum; it has a beginning and an end so far as its human aspects are concerned, but from its beginning to its end it is one, unified and continuous.

Chapter 12

HOW PERSONALITY BECOMES CHRISTIAN

IT IS A BASIC CONVICTION among Christian educators that in becoming Christian personality takes on new quality. The identity of the individual remains the same, but his spirit and life are so renewed and changed that he may in a very genuine sense think of himself as a new person.

How We Become Christian

It is clear from the writings of Paul that there is something of a dynamic tension in his thought on how he became a Christian. He definitely identifies himself with the person that he was: " For ye have heard of my conversation in time past in the Jews' religion, how that beyond measure I persecuted the church of God, and wasted it: and profited in the Jews' religion above many my equals in mine own nation, being exceedingly zealous of the traditions of my fathers " (Gal. 1: 13, 14). " If any other man thinketh that he hath whereof he might trust in the flesh, I more: circumcised the eighth day, of the stock of Israel, of the tribe of Benjamin, a Hebrew of the Hebrews; as touching the law, a Pharisee; concerning zeal, persecuting the church; touching the righteousness which is in the law, blameless " (Phil. 3: 4–6).

What is meant by the essential identity of personality, regardless of whether it is Christian or not, is this recognition that one has always been oneself. I shall always be myself, but new qualities may become characteristic of my personality so that I may well consider myself as a different person.

That was the other side of the dynamic tension in Paul's experience; he thought of himself as a new creature. " This one thing I do, forgetting those things which are behind, and reaching forth unto those things which are before, I press toward the mark for the prize of the high calling of God in Christ Jesus " (Phil. 3: 13, 14) .

He knew that he had been reborn in spirit. He had been so spiritually renewed that it was as if he had entered into the womb of experience again and had been reborn into a new kind of life. But he had a lively sense of his continuous identity, and at the same time he thought of himself as a renewed, reborn, converted, changed, redeemed, saved individual.

The sense of dynamic tension is characteristic of personality becoming Christian. When Christian personality is thought of in a developmental sense, sometimes there is a tendency to forget that there is also this sense of renewal, this sense of radical change and the achievement of new direction.

Our concern is with the religious reconstruction and transformation of personality toward the fullness of the Christian life. All the processes of Christian education find their use only in relation to this reconstruction and transformation of experience. This is Christian education's basic concern. We teach and lead through the various kinds of guided educational experience for the sake of the reconstruction and transformation of personality toward the Christian.

The individual is to recognize himself, become himself, and realize himself as a *person* in Christ. Christ is the mediator of God's reality, righteousness, love, and grace. We come to God in Christ through the Holy Spirit, who is the living and present reality of God with us and with all men. Christian experience and personality develop as through the Holy Spirit, God in Christ becomes the definitive reality in life to the child, youth, and adult. Christian personality develops to the extent that the initiative and the redeeming reality of God in Christ become the core of the individual's motivation. To be a Christian person means to live in Christ.

In the final analysis Christian personality develops as our experience is reconstructed, transformed, and redeemed by God in Christ. It develops through the experience of Christian faith, the gaining of Christian belief, and growth in the Christian way of life. Faith is integral emotion. Belief is clear intellectual analysis and commitment. The practical side is growth in the Christian way of life.

Christian personality develops through the expression of Christian values and meanings through a variety of mediums, most of them in the arts: music, drama, speech, literature, painting, sculpture, architecture, and others, but primarily in worship. The artist or writer who does not worship will have little to say with regard to Christian truth.

Christian personality develops through participation in the creation of a Christian society. He who is unconcerned about the condition of social life is fulfilling less than his full responsibility as a Christian. He is actually running the serious danger of stunting his own personal religious growth because he is failing in the active, social expression of his Christian responsibility.

The development of Christian personality is thus dependent upon the gaining of rich and profound Christian experience, the refinement of experience with the use of Christian standards, and the organization of experience for the realization of the fullness of life in Christ.

THE RELIGION OF CHILDHOOD

The religion of childhood has an integrity and value of its own, and is also preparatory to developments yet to come. The child is eager to explore religious and spiritual things. Just as in childhood there is an eagerness to explore all of experience as it expands before the child, so he is ready to live with the religious and spiritual realities about him. Any idea that is presented to him will be thought through and weighed on his level; it will be dealt with by him in terms of his experience. As he explores, his religious experience and his experience of the life of the spirit will grow.

The religion of childhood uses concrete imagery. Things mean what they are and what they say. Words come to evoke specific pictures in the mind of the child. This is very important for religious teachers because our religious teaching is full of concrete imagery to which maturity has given abstract meaning. It must be remembered that what this teaching evokes in the mind of the child is concrete images, and not the abstract truth that we conceive of when we are presented with the same ideas.

This of course points to the fact that we do a great deal of our religious teaching too early. For instance, we do not wait for a period of intellectual readiness for doctrinal instruction. If a child becomes a member of the church at the age of twelve, he has been given some prior doctrinal instruction. But a great many children are not able to handle abstractions at this age, and doctrine is replete with abstractions. Probably up to one half of our young people of twelve are not able to handle them at all.

Religious belief in childhood is earnest but tends to be naïve. "When I was a child, I spake as a child, I understood as a child, I thought as a child" (I Cor. 13:11). This is a recognition of the fact that the child does think about these things, and earnestly, but on his own level. The child has rather profound beliefs, but they are not likely to be very coherent or consistent. We should conserve the sincerity and conviction of the child, but in the nurture of his religious life change naïve, childish, and inadequate belief into mature, adult, adequate, and competent belief.

Religion in childhood often includes the attitude and experience of wonder and awe. All one has to do to be convinced of this is to watch the child's intuitive reverence as he is confronted with some new experience. This again is the kind of experience we want to conserve and develop.

Childish faith must grow up, but may remain properly childlike. What we mean is that it is a simple faith; but if it were childish, one could not live by it as an adult. If it is childlike, then it conserves the earnestness, the eagerness, the wonder, and the awe of the child's experience, but is transformed into something that is adequate for adult life. This points up the need for growth, development, reconstruction, and transformation of experience through all of life.

THE RELIGION OF YOUTH

What is a youth like when he is being religious? The experience of the young person, the person in his teens, is one of sincere search. He has seldom found what he feels is final for him.

He will have had experience in which he has committed himself, but he is still searching to find out what that commitment means in all the aspects of his life. It does not dawn on him immediately what all its implications are. So even though he has come early to a commitment to the Christian faith and life, to Jesus Christ himself, nevertheless the rest of his youth will have within it the experience of finding out what it means to live the Christian life.

It follows from the nature of childish belief, and the expanding experience of youth, that youth will involve a redefinition of the object of religious belief. When I was a child I thought about God in concrete fashion, not in abstract terms. Now I must revise my concept, so as to understand him in mature terms. It takes a long period of redefinition to come to espouse such a simple yet complex definition as, " God is love." It is highly abstract because of what God is and what love is. It is a definition that keeps opening itself up to us in larger and larger circles of meaning as our experience expands to be able to comprehend it.

It would be interesting for one to write down all that God means to him: what he thinks God is; how God deals with him; what his response to God should be. Then let him put the notes away and come back to them after a period of years after having done the same exercise again. Comparing the two he would see how his idea of God, his definition of the object of belief, had changed.

Youth is the point at which we come to understand the relationship between God and Jesus Christ. It takes a great deal of redefinition of the concept of God to realize the bond between

Christ the Son and God the Father. The problem, if this is taught too early, is that of identifying the concrete imagery of Jesus with the full nature of God. Our Christology has to be as large as our idea of the nature, will, purpose, and reality of God himself. As God is defined in terms of his revelation to us in Jesus Christ or the movement of his Spirit within our hearts, society, and the universe, a very profound process of redefinition is involved.

Youth experiences the enrichment and expansion of commitments. The child is likely to be loyal to his friends and to his family. As he grows his commitments should become more inclusive. His loyalties are enriched and expanded until they reach the climax of commitment to God himself.

The religion of youth is often passionate in its loyalties. They are richer and more extended than those of childhood, but are still limited in scope, because the experience of the youth has not developed to the point where they can be inclusive. But they are passionately held. Think, for instance, of the devotion that high school young people give to the team. Adults look at this kind of loyalty and wonder how it is possible. They ask why young people cannot see things in proper perspective: " Can't you see that this isn't all there is in life? "

But in a way it *is* all there is in life for the time being. The adult exclaims: " But this is so limited! It doesn't represent what life really is all about." But there it is: passionate, intense loyalty.

Even though youth's commitment to Christ is of necessity upon the basis of limited experience, it is consuming in its intensity. Notice the conflicts that arise in the church between lukewarm adults and enthusiastic young people. Here is a key to youth work. If we are so " mature " that we have tempered our loyalty to Jesus Christ, we are less than fitted for youth work, for there we must be able to match the passionate spirit of youth.

The intellectual side of the matter is the intense conviction of youth. The convictions that youth holds are held intensely even though they may be somewhat limited in scope compared with what they will be when maturity is attained. There is experimentation with beliefs in action. When a new belief, conviction, or loyalty dawns upon the youth, he tries it out. As he puts it into action and experiments with it, he will find out how valid it is and how well it works.

THE RELIGION OF MATURITY

What is religion like in maturity? Maturity in the religious life is characterized by poised receptivity. The child explores; the youth searches; the adult in the religious life is receptive to new experience. He is not likely to be so indiscriminate about it as are children and youth, but he knows that nature and God have more to teach than he already knows.

The religion of adulthood involves discrimination in values. The child or youth is likely to look upon values in a rather heterogeneous fashion. The adult is definitely trying to build these values into a pattern that will focus them upon his goal.

One might say that adulthood is thus characterized centrally by the achievement of perspective in religion. God, nature, society, and the individual himself are seen in perspective by the religious adult.

Adulthood seeks integrity in religious experience. Why is integrity such a troublesome problem? We are continually being accused of, and accusing ourselves of, hypocrisy. We are plagued by feelings of guilt and remorse, with failure to achieve our best. Whenever this is the case, we feel that we lack integrity.

How may belief become the core of Christian integrity? The experience process raises at least three questions about human direction, the answers to which become fused into beliefs. What is feasible? We do not believe what is not feasible. What is possible? We do not believe what is not possible. What is desirable or valuable? We do not believe what is lacking in value or desirability. Our beliefs will, in the long run, express and integrate the answers that we give to these three questions.

Adulthood thus knows some certainty of belief about the will of God. This belief centers in such areas as the need for the religious life, strict adherence to truth, and the validity of the principle of love. It is when we violate such beliefs as these that we feel that we lack integrity.

The religious adult speaks the language of religion with meaning and conviction. The child experiments with the language of religion, as does the youth. What does grace mean? What does redemption mean? What do we mean by the Spirit? He is trying to find out and experimenting to discover. The adult uses such language with sincerity born of experience.

In adulthood there is focused commitment. That is, the loyalties we hold are not limited as in youth. They are, as it were, complete (although they are never really complete). The adult has a steady sense of purpose, direction, and meaning. He has a much more unified goal than the child or youth can have.

As youth experimented with beliefs in action, so adulthood experiences social effectiveness. The adult has become skilled in carrying out in action such beliefs as righteousness, justice, love, and truth. If he has not, if he has turned them into objects of hypocritical lip service rather than objects of belief in action, he has blundered onto a dangerous byway in the religious life.

The adult knows fulfillment. He finds it in prayer, worship, and in creative participation in the fellowship of the Church.

Chapter 13

EDUCATION FOR THE LIFE IN CHRIST

WE ARE ENGAGED in education for the life in Christ. This differentiates the things that we do from many other types of education that may be generally moral or religious. It points directly to what we are trying to do: so to remake, remold, transform, and reconstruct the experience of the children, youth, and adults with whom we live and work that they will experience their lives as the life in Christ.

The aim is that the living Christ shall take hold of life. As adults we know something of the meaning of the life in Christ. We realize it in our prayer, worship, church life, and community life. But what of the child, the youth, and the person outside the Church who knows little or nothing of God in Christ? This is the question of how education for the life in Christ takes place.

EDUCATION AND CHRISTIAN EDUCATION

Broadly speaking, education takes place in all the individual's relationships. There is no experience that I have that does not have some effect upon me to change me.

I stay one person, whole and unified. I have a sense of continuity from early childhood to the present, which I project even into the future. Experience and memory serve me well. I have a real sense of identity. I identify myself with the child and youth that I was, and with the person I am to become.

But the world keeps impinging on me. Things keep happening to me. I think, read, work, play, pray, worship, go to meetings, take trips, teach classes, live with my family, and a thou-

118

sand and one other things. These flood in on my life. It changes as these new demands, opportunities, and challenges open up before me. In fact, once in a while an idea occurs to me that revolutionizes my whole thinking and way of life. Old habits go; I take on new ones. I can become a new person. I can be, as it were, born again.

These things happen in the life stream of my experience. They happen in the life stream of the experience of the children, youth, and adults with whom we work in Christian education day by day, week by week, and year after year.

Those who have taught in the church school or who have led in some other phase of Christian education work can look back over the years upon profound things that have happened in the lives of the young people that they have taught. Perhaps they were not even aware at the time of what was taking place. Often they know only from later testimony that what they did affected the experience of some young person and changed him so that he became a new person with new direction.

To the extent that the relationships that make up a person's life are permeated with the realization of the living Christ, Christian education takes place. It is thus that education for the life in Christ begins and continues in human life.

We have definite responsibility for certain of these relationships. As parents we may make Christ real, or we may deny him to our children. To the extent that we make Christ real in the life of the home, Christian education may take place there. As church school teachers and leaders, we may make Christ real, or we may caricature him, to the children with whom we deal. As public-school teachers, we may be living examples of the life in Christ, and the schoolroom may, without the speaking of sectarian words, become an example of the Christian way of life. As citizens, in the life of the community and nation, we have a responsibility for living and making manifest the life in Christ, as well as experimenting diligently to discover what it means in specific terms for the citizen in the community and nation.

I know something of the duration and quality of my relationships with others. As a parent, teacher, friend, neighbor, and community leader, to what extent and how is the life that I lead permeated with the realization of the living Christ? To what extent and how are the relationships that I bear likewise permeated with the imperative of his living presence?

This is not to bespeak a totally controlled environment. We do not become Christian, as it were, brick on brick through some automatic system of controlled conditioning. Neither is it wise to shelter children too much. Too much sheltering produces weakness where strength is acutely needed. One of the ways in which we grow in the life in Christ is to be guided and taught by those who know Christ, but then to go out into life and meet the challenges, resistances, and opposition that will inevitably be found there. It is then that we test out and prove our ideas, doctrines, convictions, and relationships. It is there that we find out that we know or do not know the strength, power, and undergirding of God in Christ. Nothing could be more alien to Christian education than to try to keep the child away from reality, to keep him completely away from suffering, to blind him to evil, or to blind him to sin. This would be actually to frustrate Christian education, for it is in meeting these forthrightly and maturely, each of us on his own level of experience, that we come really to find and test the profundities of the life in Christ. If we help others to meet Christ on the way, in the home, school, community, or club, then those with whom we work may become agents of the redeeming Christ themselves when they come face to face with aspects of life that are not Christian.

THE PRACTICE OF CHRISTIAN EDUCATION

As we carry education for the life in Christ into practice, what will it be like? Each leader sees his task within his own context, defined by his own particular responsibilities. What about the practice of Christian education in these relationships? Each of us is engaged in some kind of Christian education in the home, community, church school, weekday school, or elsewhere, and will think of it in that context. Some are members or officers in some group in the church. Even these are carrying on Christian education, because telling influences are there for the life in Christ.

Here, then, are some of the specifics. Our leaders will grow in their own experience of Christ. They will be persons who spend time in study of the Bible, the Christian faith, and Christian work in today's world. They will spend time in Christian service and action, and in Christian fellowship, an experience that is much neglected in our day. They will spend much time in worship, by themselves and with others.

The Christian leader will also grow in the life in Christ himself by looking upon his own teaching, leadership, or membership as an opportunity to become personally more Christian, to find out for himself more of what it means to live in Christ. He will keep questions like this before him: What is my aim this week, or this year, so far as my own Christian growth is concerned? His major question may well be this: How may my leadership in this group help us together to grow in the life in Christ?

Our enterprise will be conducted in the spirit of the living Christ. We will seek to express there our abiding relationship with him, our realization of his spirit and purpose. Relationships between officers, teachers, and pupils will be carried on in this spirit. This will do away with the illogical and defeating dualism in which we teach in the curriculum the Christian way of love, and practice in the administration of the enterprise an autocratic way of arbitrary power.

When our enterprise is permeated with the spirit of the living Christ, there is a strength and reality about it that will not let the teacher do less than his best, nor the young person that which is not in keeping with its spirit. There will be discipline, self-discipline, and the discipline of Christian love seeking nurture within order. Christian education in its practice and administration seeks to incarnate the love of God in Christ. What love means in many cases is to remind the individual of what he can be, what he must be, and what in Christ he may be.

It is difficult to be Christian in these days. Many of the difficulties involved will be encountered in the life of the class, the school, or in their administration. Part of the task is to provide the setting for the solution of just such difficulties. Thus in a sense the life of the enterprise itself may become the curriculum.

Teacher training will seek to develop teaching skills that will give ever more effective expression to our mutual search for the Christian truth and way of life. It will stress training in the life of the spirit — not just, " What do I do with these children? " but, " How may I become the kind of person who can do the kind of job that needs to be done? " Training will emphasize methods, but more; it will emphasize the qualities of the teacher's own life. It will stress becoming Christian as well as learning to teach.

Our churches and schools will be viewed as part of the Church of the living Christ. Each class *is* the Church of the living Christ. All members are a part of it; this is the spirit in which they gather. Church school is one of the ways in which He comes into our midst and becomes the guiding motive of all that we do.

In his spirit we will seek to minister to all, and to see those we work with as individuals. Educational evangelism must be concerned, not just with those within our constituency, but with the whole community. We will seek to minister to those we reach in terms of their own needs and experiences. Our objectives and plans for any class, or any period will be determined in a spirit of togetherness in Christ.

We will teach the Bible in order that it may become the living Word to our pupils. We will teach the Christian faith as meaningful to their lives. We will teach about the Church and its history so that they may see themselves as part of its purpose and history. We will engage in deeds of loving service, and like projects, so that Christian ethical motives may be experienced and tested. We will teach prayer and worship in order that we may together know the profundities of living experience of the Christ.

We will teach Christian truth creatively in order that it may be rediscovered and understood: in order that it may genuinely become the pupil's through his own experience of it, and not merely something he has learned to please or satisfy us. The

Christian faith must be experienced to be known. Creative experience in communicating and appropriating it at each level of experience is the means by which it becomes known in a living way by generation after generation. Mere mechanical transmission is likely to kill the spirit, while creative rediscovery produces the atmosphere in which the Christian faith may take root and grow.

We will seek the co-operation of every other person and agency ministering to our young people. We may not be too successful in some of our attempts at co-ordination of the educational influences that bear upon them, yet interpretation to the home, school, informal educational agencies, and any others of importance will at least indicate to them the integrating concept of Christian education that is the basis for our enterprise. The result may be greater readiness for co-operation. It may even be a conscious attempt to help to interpret to the young person the unity or correlation of aim that may easily come to characterize the impact of all these agencies upon him.

We will take our Christian education duties seriously, realizing that the program must be adequately housed, equipped, financed, and administered. We will take specific steps to provide more adequately for these necessities. This will mean that we interpret our aims, accomplishments, and needs accurately to those whose responsibility it is to provide these things. In this, the enterprise becomes the obligation of the whole Church, not that of just a few interested individuals.

We will judge our success by the degree to which personalities are transformed and reconstructed toward the spirit of Christ and the Christian way of life, and the degree to which the reality of the living Christ takes hold of purposes and lives.

Education for the life in Christ takes place when Christ is the motive, guide, and judge of every educational relationship. The Christian educator, himself experiencing new life in Christ, seeks to translate this reality into the specific needs and opportunities of the educational enterprise, that it may effectively undertake to represent the Christ in the church and community.

Part Four

SPECIFIC CONCERNS

Chapter 14

PLANNING THE CURRICULUM

CURRICULUM is essentially a process of the reordering of experience. The curriculum of Christian education seeks to reorder experience so that it may become Christian in quality. It consists of all the experiences selected, organized, and used to achieve our educational aims.

The nature of curriculum of Christian education is summed up in Coe's classic statement of curriculum theory:

"A curriculum is not primarily a systematic set of ideas, but a progressive order of motives actually at work, actually fruiting here and now. The elements that have to be considered may be stated in a chain as follows:

"(a) To help the pupil to experience growing communion with God.

"(b) In and through growing human fellowships in the family, the church, and elsewhere.

"(c) Fellowship in the act of worship, with the help of music and the other arts.

"(d) And in constructive and remedial social activities.

"(e) Which include the missionary enterprise, but expand it.

"(f) All of which requires constant and growing discrimination, foresight, and deliberation.

"(g) And for this reason calls for illumination from Scripture, history, doctrines, science, current events, and the creations of imagination" (George Albert Coe, *A Social Theory of Religious Education*, p. 98. Charles Scribner's Sons, 1917).

CURRICULUM PRINCIPLES

There are certain educational principles fundamental to the curriculum:

Learning takes place through experience.

The curriculum consists of selected experiences.

The curriculum consists of rich and varied experiences, selected on the basis of two kinds of criteria: developmental and Christian.

Perception is involved. We are endowed with, and may develop to the point of proficiency, the ability to perceive what is outside ourselves. This is the basis of human experience, the elemental interaction between the individual and his environment. The curriculum includes exploring and discovering and the reordering and guidance of human experience in terms of the perceptions thus gained.

Conception is involved: the accumulation of the individual's experience, the totality of his reorganized, meaningful perceptions. Perceptions, as they are reorganized into meaningful concepts, expand experience.

The heritage of experience is involved. The experience of the community, society, the Church, and the general culture defines our tradition. The curriculum re-creates the Christian tradition in the pupil's experience. It also asks how experience within this culture may be so reorganized and redeemed that it may become Christian.

The curriculum has the task of taking us from where we are to a new level of accomplishment where we have gained valuable experience. Therefore it is grounded upon perception, accumulated individual experience, and the accumulated experience of the community and culture.

The problem of education is to re-create in the individual the experience of the group. The child coming into the world has to contact the experience of the race, rediscover it, and make it his own. In our culture this includes the creative personal rediscovery of the experience of the Church and the Christian faith.

However, the principle of selectivity has to be used. Everything that has taken place in the past cannot be remembered or re-created. We are interested only in re-creating what has central significance and is most real. The principle of selectivity in Christian education curriculum implies criteria like these:

> Those experiences will be selected which provide the basis for the emotional learnings that underlie Christian experience and Christian living.
>
> Those experiences will be selected which provide the basis for those knowledges, skills, and understandings necessary for Christian experience and Christian living.
>
> Those experiences will be selected which will acquaint the individual with those aspects of general experience which are most likely to have religious implications. While the Christian life involves new and special kinds of experiences, it also involves the redemption of old experiences and general experience.
>
> Those experiences will be selected which will acquaint the individual with the distinctively Christian aspects of experience.
>
> Those experiences will be selected which will provide the basis for appropriate commitments at the various levels of experience.
>
> Those experiences will be selected which will encourage development of deliberation, reflection, insight, prayer, and worship.

THE COMPONENTS OF CURRICULUM

Four kinds of experiences are included in the curriculum. These components have been developed previously: guided study, action in social reconstruction, fellowship and recreation, and worship. Experiences of these types will be selected in terms of the criteria mentioned above, so that they may lead to ideas, values, beliefs, behaviors, commitments, and habits that are Christian and that are appropriate to the developmental level of the pupil.

All four — guided study, action, fellowship, and worship — have to be included in the experience of the individual and the group; development is stunted if rich experiences in all four areas are not provided. All such experiences must of course be appropriately graded.

The church cannot provide all the experiences that the pupil needs. Neither can the parents. The application of the same criteria to the four types of experience will make the responsibility of the church and the home clear.

NEW DEVELOPMENTS

How far have we come in the development of the curriculum of Christian education? Two major steps have recently been taken. There is no doubt among responsible curriculum people that it is to be developed educationally. There is little feeling that it is to be developed outside an experience context. Formerly, the curriculum was likely to be built entirely in terms of Biblical content, logically or chronologically presented, or in terms of logical doctrinal sequence. Now the primary norms are educational. What kinds of instruction in the Bible are appropriate for those who use the materials? What doctrinal questions are appropriate to be raised at the various levels of development?

The argument between experience and content as emphases in the curriculum has virtually ended. Twenty years ago, as explained in the first chapter, this was a real source of conflict. There were curriculums that were content-centered, not taking experiential norms into account. On the other hand, there were curriculums that were experience-centered, where content was used only to facilitate and enrich the reconstruction of the experience of the individual. Since the International Council of Religious Education's 1946–1947 Study of Christian Education this discussion has largely ended, and it is assumed in all curriculum writing that experience and content are both important ingredients. The conflict has largely been resolved and the principle adopted that content, in order to be learned, has to be used in an experience framework. Content is determinative, but is meaningfully appropriated in the developing experience of the pupil.

Creative work in curriculum construction has been done lately by various denominations. With the aim of complete revision, the Protestant Episcopal Church has set about in a six-volume study to define what the Church must teach. Written for adults, these volumes are attempts to define essential content. When they are completed, their findings may be given to people who are age-level specialists in Christian education for study and action on their curriculum implications.

The Presbyterian Church in the U.S.A. has completely revised its curriculum by asking: What do the Bible, Christian doctrine, and the Christian life mean in experiential terms to the children, young people, and adults by whom the curriculum is to be used? What experiences are essential in order that they may appropriate Biblical truth, understand and believe Christian doctrine, and live the Christian life? This is experience related to basic content.

The great gains that were made early in the century in making the experience of the pupil the matrix of the educational process are being conserved, but are now being used in such a way as to prevent that experience from becoming just an anarchy of muddled content. There is a complete recognition of the fact that the context is experiential, and a clear definition of what the experience process should produce in content learned.

SOME NEEDED DEVELOPMENTS

What still remains to be done in curriculum? The curriculum process, while it is understood well at the denominational level, is still baffling to many local church teachers. Their question is, What, now that it is in my hands, am I supposed to do to use it effectively? This is an acute problem in supervision, one that still has to be solved.

Another problem awaits solution: Can curriculums be developed in terms of the various types of local churches we actually have rather than on the assumption that all the churches within a denomination should use the same materials? While a great deal of research must be done before we are ready to solve this problem, some steps in this direction have already been taken. Some denominations now plan some of their materials for use outside their own churches, knowing that local churches that find the materials suitable to their needs will be interested in using them, regardless of denomination. A Methodist church is as a rule not too different from a Congregational or Presbyterian church in the same community. There are often greater differences between the churches of the same denomination in different communities and regions than there are between the churches of various denominations within the same community or region. Research must be applied to the questions: What types of situations exist? What kinds of church schools do we have? What different sorts of needs must the curriculum of Christian education seek to meet? If we were to classify them, we might discover that we have something like a dozen basic types of Christian education situations.

Curriculum might be prepared in terms of these types of situations. If an interdenominational approach were made to the problem, each denomination could easily supplement its curriculum with the materials that it particularly wants to have taught.

A further problem is well on the way to solution, that of the use of the Bible in the curriculum. Two questions that have to be resolved may merely be mentioned: When and how is the Bible to be taught as content? When and how is it to be taught as the revealed Word of God?

Individualizing the Curriculum

The curriculum is only as good as what happens to the student as the result of its use. Therefore it should be built and judged in large part in terms of individual use. What guides may be used to individualize it?

Plan for each student. What we receive in printed form are sets of curriculum suggestions. They become a curriculum in fact when they are used in terms of the needs, interests, and desires of each individual pupil.

Teach in terms of what the student can and wants to use now and as he looks ahead. This is the central principle of adaptation of the curriculum to individual differences and individual needs.

Start with each student where his present knowledge stops.

Deal in large units, but remember that each must consist of specific detail well organized. Do not be too worried about the many specific things that the individual is supposed to learn. It is more important for him to get major points and be moved to find out more about them for himself — to become so urgently concerned about them that he will read, study, explore, and act.

Seek to bring together the loose ends in the student's thinking. Work toward organization, meaning, and unity.

Seek to establish and maintain a unified and directional concept of his work in the student's mind.

Anticipate — be adequately prepared for each new step.

THE LOCAL CHURCH AND ITS CURRICULUM

What is the responsibility of the local church for the administration of the curriculum? It is to determine for itself what its curriculum content shall be. It will seek help from the best curriculum thinking that has been done. But even if it adopts a curriculum that is already prepared, a careful analytical study is needed to make clear to all the workers what the content is and each one's function in teaching it.

It is also the church's responsibility in the administration of the curriculum to know the specific experiences basic to and available within the community.

On the basis of these findings it is the church's responsibility intelligently to select those specific materials and experiences which will constitute the curriculum through which the church will seek to meet the needs of its people for Christian experience and Christian faith.

Chapter 15

METHODS ARE TOOLS

IN THE CHURCH SCHOOL and in other aspects of the Christian education program, various tools are at our disposal. They are to be used to build Christian personality and create the Christian community. There is no other compelling reason for their use. If they will not get the job done, then other tools must be found and put to work.

Variety is called for. Constant repetition of a single method does not accomplish the task effectively as a rule. If the child knows that the same method will be used every Sunday, the process loses taste for him. Variety is needed to provide the many approaches necessary to experience.

As various methods are discussed in this chapter, there will be those mentioned which you have used in the church school or home. But recognize that there may be others suggested that might enrich, expand, and make more fruitful and competent the teaching you do as minister, parent, teacher, or supervisor.

DIRECT INSTRUCTION

Serious guided study involves direct instruction. Although instruction may be the specific aim, both formal and informal methods are required. Creative methods, involving self-expression and group planning in terms of self-defined goals, are indispensable.

Discussion is used for purposes of clarification, pupil response, and the creative give-and-take of ideas. Speakers and consultants are called in on subjects that lend themselves to treatment by experts. Use is made of movies, filmstrips, and records that are both fascinating and enlightening. Having students prepare their own audio-visuals and talks and conduct their own discussions teaches them how to plan and work out experiences of creative and co-operative group study.

Direct instruction implies Christian subject matter. How could Christian education be carried on without the Bible, Christian hymns, the literature that is our heritage in the Christian faith, and the use of Christian teachings and doctrine?

But subject matter other than Christian is also used. A father and mother are deeply troubled because they had inquired of their teen-age daughter what she was taking up in church school and were told that the previous Sunday there had been a lesson on Confucianism. They asked, " Since there is so little time for Bible study, why take the time to teach about Confucianism and the other religions? " It was explained that the girl had begun to ask questions about other people's religions, and that it was time to make clear to her the relation between the other living religions and Christianity. We use other than Christian subject matter, not because we are trying to do the whole job of education with our children, but because they need and have a right to see the Christian faith and life in relation to other aspects of their living.

The findings and methods of science are considered in order to help the pupil to relate them to the Christian faith, so that he does not in immature fashion make science do the work of philosophy and religion as well as perform its own legitimate functions.

Thus the pupil sees the rest of his life in Christian perspective. We guide him in the church and home that he may learn his science and history as a Christian, break into his new job as a Christian, and go to his parties and on his dates as a Christian. Being Christian colors his whole approach to knowledge and experience.

If we keep other kinds of subject matter out of our Christian teaching, he will inevitably get the impression either that the Christian faith has nothing to say about these things, or is boxed off in some corner of his life where it has little or no relevance.

In that case, he will become not a confirmed Christian but a confirmed secularist. He will look upon his education, business, and social life as separate from his religion. The job of the Christian religion in catching up and transforming all of life will not be done.

It is not too strong to say that direct instruction cannot be successful without creative participation by the student and teacher in its accomplishment. Fundamental to creative discovery, appropriation, and re-creation of ideas are such methods as systematic inquiry, self-evaluation, and group evaluation. These are more than optional methods to be casually applied. They are disciplines, skills, that require training and practice. Their mastery is the condition to be met in order that thinking may be fruitfully creative.

A Sampling of Methods

Play is the work of the little child. Creative play, games, even sports are used in the program. They are most important for learning certain social attitudes and elements of character. In them the individual is enabled to unbend, relax, become friendly, and enter into fellowship. Especially with the tiny child, to play creatively and enjoyably in the church school or the weekday church nursery school leads him to certain newness of life and also to love and identify himself with the church.

Old-fashioned stereotyped handwork is rapidly being replaced by really creative activities. Too often in the crowded church school we settle for less. If we suggest that the child paint or crayon, we can at least help him to develop and express his own ideas in his own way. Creativity says, even when the child is crowded in, " Get an idea and say it your own way, or draw or paint it your own way." The teacher is there to help the child to develop his ideas, even rudimentary ones, and to provide the conditions within which in creative fashion he may express them. Let him select his own colors, make up his own form, or work out his own composition. Then it is his own, says what he means, and is thus creative.

While it is difficult to use dramatics in some of our church schools, the most useful form of educational dramatics, creative or classroom dramatics, does not require a great deal of space or elaborate properties. What happens in making up a play and acting it? The individual who takes part identifies himself with the character and tries out new ideas in tentative practice. He tends to feel like the person he is portraying, experience what that person experienced, speak like him, and believe as he believed. One fruitful thing to do in the church and home is to take the parts of persons that we seek to know or identify ourselves with. Children act out parts by themselves when they are unaware of others. They emulate people they have seen, imitate people with whom they identify themselves, or work through situations with dramatic imagination. A simple and effective method is to read great drama together, a method easily used in the church and home.

We use music, grading it to the understanding and enjoyment of the child. While we use it in the normal course of events in the church school, why should we not use it at home also? A parent secures a copy of the primary hymnal, and after the supper dishes are done plays for a few minutes some of the hymns that her child is learning in Sunday school. It is a natural sort of thing; the child may be playing in the room, seemingly not paying attention. But he may come and sing along with her. Occasionally she uses a new hymn. Informal and spontaneous singing, creative music in the home and church school, do not require that we be great musicians; we only have to enjoy and value the fellowship of singing together. In connection with music we sometimes use rhythms. Rhythms involve the use of the body to express feelings and tell stories dramatically and beautifully, with music helping the interpretation.

Trips and excursions are part of the program. We visit churches, and see things that are of historic and community interest, thus enriching the educational experience.

Group methods of various sorts are used, including what is called " group dynamics," for we know that there are many mat-

ters in which our children's friends are more effective teachers
than we are. In addition to developing group responsibility, the
kind of education that takes place rather spontaneously among
our children and their friends is of a sort that will help them to
grow into the Christian life.

Students are learning to take responsibility and leadership for
themselves. There was a time when every worship service was led
by the superintendent. Student participation was limited to carefully memorized " pieces." Students are now learning to plan and
lead in worship. Much of our classwork is based on reports that
students present. Student councils and youth councils are being
organized in the church school and youth fellowship in order that
young people may learn the skills of responsible leadership. If
they thus learn them, they are likely to grow up into responsible
Christian adulthood; if they do not learn these skills, always do
only what they are told or are asked to do and nothing more, the
possibilities are lessened of their growing into responsible adulthood.

Activities are often organized into projects, units with specific
purposes that set off the meaning of the activities. The aim of a
project usually is to explore an area or solve a problem. It inte-
grates a variety of activities into itself in accomplishing its purpose.

Evangelism is the method of bringing children, youth, and
adults to make decisions for the Christian life on their own.
When they are skilled in decision-making in a variety of life situations, they may be ready to take that climactic step in which they
can say, " I am a Christian; I dedicate myself without reserve to
Jesus Christ as my Redeemer, Saviour, and Guide." This should
be the beginning of a grown-up Christian experience that is real,
full, and rich. When it comes, it is thought of, not so much as a
decision that one makes of himself, but as a free personal response
to God's call to him in Christ.

Take just a few short glimpses more at the home. The child
brings books home from church school. Think what it means to
him to see his parent, without any prodding, sit down and read

them for himself. Some books are designed to be read to the child. But what is meant here is simply that parents are interested enough to read them themselves. The fellowship of perfectly natural questions may very easily follow.

Parents can co-operate in meaningful participation by youth in camps and conferences. If an anticipation is aroused of the important experiences that await them, and if when they come home we help them not to feel the letdown that might follow that mountaintop experience, we have helped their Christian growth.

Occasionally even relaxed roughhouse becomes a method by which we come closer to one another and by which we may unbend and open up the possibilities for fellowship that underlie the whole process of Christian education.

The "Why" of Method

The individual as he works and responds in a variety of situations, and through a variety of methods, helps us better to understand his needs and channel his abilities.

Using a variety of methods in the church school and in the home creates a readiness for Christian experience. The use of a rich variety of methods leads the individual to readiness for Christian experience. He reaches out for new experience of many kinds, including and focusing upon Christian experience.

By using certain of these methods he finds his way of unbending, of becoming himself at his best. He may find out for himself how to work with other people.

The individual may become specifically and voluntarily Christian by participating as a Christian in the activities of a Christian fellowship. The church and the home may be such fellowships. Methods in the church and home are processes, dynamic in character, through which the personal, the social, and the divine integrate to promote growth in Christian living. This means that Christian personality, Christian character, Christian understanding, and Christian responsibility may come into being.

Chapter 16

WHERE RESPONSIBILITY LIES

WHERE DOES RESPONSIBILITY LIE in Christian education? We tend to divide responsibility as it should not be divided. We analyze, but effectiveness depends upon looking at the task as a whole. Christian education as a process can be seen best when it is looked at in its entirety. The church, the home, the school, and the community are all responsible for it. The task is not likely to be done unless there is real co-operation among them.

THE INDIVIDUAL HIMSELF

Final responsibility for Christian education lies with the individual himself. When we are dealing with people in Christian education, it is of extreme importance to remember that ultimately they know and are responsible for themselves. It is the student, the pupil, the individual himself who is being educated. In the long run he may take or leave what we have to say; he may take or leave the kinds of experience we offer him. He will do the job of choosing and selecting; he will build his own experience so that it will have meaning for him.

The individual is set in motion, and learning may take place, when new experience tends to throw him to some extent off balance. One of the principles of education that we have used before is that it takes place where there is tension, problem, question, or interest.

What do such experiences do for us? We come up to certain experiences, as it were, with our minds made up; we have a sense of knowing our way, of having direction. The new experience to some degree destroys this harmony, stability, and inner unity. What do we do about it? We try instinctively to re-create the balance again, to pull ourselves back into the harmony and inner unity that have been destroyed. But it is never possible to be quite the same again. Each new balance, harmony, or unity as it is achieved means a somewhat altered self and personality. As the process comes to its new climax, we are able to say, and to feel profoundly, " I am one with myself again; I am no longer fragmented in spirit; I am one in purpose, in aim, and in ideal."

This goes on all the time. Every new experience has to be assimilated or rejected in some fashion. The processes of assimilation and rejection of experience are necessary to integrity and to sanity.

Teachers provide new experiences all the time for their pupils; parents provide them for their children; the neighborhood provides them; God provides them for us and for those with whom we associate. All these experiences have to be lived with, evaluated, and used in the re-creation of the inner unity and integrity that we cannot do without. This the clue to the decisive responsibility that each individual has in becoming Christian. It points clearly to the fact that for him the process is primarily one of continuity and unity of experience.

But look at Christian education as it is carried on in actual practice, from the point of view of the persons and groups who are the educators, and the picture is quite different. Clearly, it should not be so. But there is no area so fragmented, so little unified, as this. There are so many persons and groups providing educational experiences for the individual, formally or informally, consciously or unconsciously, but always with a striking lack of co-ordination of plan and effort, that for the individual the process may easily become utterly bewildering.

The principle of co-ordination in Christian education upon which we may act and upon which a successful educational practice may be based is the religious principle of complete commitment and loyalty to the highest. If every person and group engaged in education were to use this principle, a high degree of co-ordination would result. Even though the public school may not indoctrinate in sectarian fashion, it is generally recognized that the success of its enterprise depends upon adherence to this principle, expressed in moral and spiritual terms. To Christians, complete commitment and loyalty mean commitment and loyalty to God in Christ, the living Christ, present in spirit with us, guiding, controlling, and motivating. The Christian use of this principle of co-ordination will achieve a high degree of unity for Christian education where there has been merely a bewildering variety of educational opportunity and endeavor.

THE HOME

Aside from the individual himself, the home has most to do with Christian education. Here it takes place most effectively. It is a fact that the values that the home actually espouses and by which it lives are most likely to be communicated almost unconsciously and incorporated into the life fabric of the child. As parents, we delegate the responsibility for the meeting of our children's spiritual needs to any other agency at great peril.

What is important is what the home really is, that is, its atmosphere, what it does from day to day, the kind of behavior that characterizes it, and the kind of activities that take place within it. All these point directly to the importance of the religious values that the parents hold, by which the home's atmosphere and character are determined.

What these values are for us in each home is the crucial question that we face. It is said that our value system is revealed by what we put in our date books and by the checks we write. These are not only indications of the way we use our time and money, but also of the values that determine their use.

Several years ago in a vacation church school in the suburbs a unit on Christian co-operation was used with a group of primary children. It was a fine unit, but it failed. Why? The people who lived in that community had come up the economic ladder the hard way. They were successes in the business world; living in that community was a badge of their success. Their values, unconsciously permeating their homes, were the values of success in the competitive struggle. Is it any wonder that a unit on co-operation failed with their children?

What are our religious habits? What do the practices of the home say in deeds as well as words to its children and youth? There are churches where the parents (the men usually well dressed in sports clothes) bring their children to church school on Sunday morning, driving them to the church, letting them out at the curb, driving off, and in another hour re-enacting the scene to gather them up. What does the child learn from this? He is likely to learn that going to church and church school is properly for children. He may well decide that when he grows up and gets to be like Daddy, he will no longer attend. Is this what we want our unconscious instruction to say to our children?

This is less than full responsibility on the part of parents. It indicates that the Christian Church does not seem very valuable to them.

Among religious practices advocated for the home, devotions are usually included. But many parents have found it difficult to use them. How may parents start to use devotions with their families? Every home will probably have a somewhat different pattern. Each home should develop the kind of devotional practice and atmosphere that has integrity for its members. We cannot engage in a practice because it is good for the children when it does not ring true for us.

If it is difficult to start sharing on the religious level, why not start at first on the intellectual level or the level of activities? Families that do things together begin to enjoy one another, and the barriers of misunderstanding between their members begin to crumble. On the intellectual side we can share our ideas: the new ideas that keep coming to us, and the abiding ideas that have great meaning for us. Why not start here, on the secular side of life? Discovering what has genuineness for us here, we may then move on to genuine religious sharing.

Each parent might start studying the Bible for himself. He might begin a vital practice of private prayer. These, with planning, will in time spill over into the life of the family in genuine and sincere fashion. If we do not study the Bible, if we do not pray, if we do not think on religious things, devotions in the family are likely to be a mere form. Each family must establish a spiritual diet for itself that is suited to its needs.

One of the ways to get started with religion in the home is to deal perfectly genuinely with the questions that children raise. Parents are too often, of course, prone to answer questions where they might better guide children in finding answers for themselves. There are questions too where they should indicate freely that they do not know the answers. The first real glimpse of God that many children have is when they realize that Father and Mother have to look beyond themselves to a power greater than they are for their answers. There is a glimpse of God beyond, in the life of the parents.

Some of the most important questions for Christian education in the home are these: What does being Christian mean to us as parents? To what extent have we achieved a fellowship of deep sharing as Christian parents? What should being a Christian mean to the child at each level of his experience? What may being a Christian mean for him in concrete terms? What should he know and do about the Bible, prayer, ethical living, belief, and service and action as a Christian? What specific steps may we take as a family to guide the practice of the Christian life in the home, the community, and beyond?

Perhaps we may reach the place where Christian nurture is looked at realistically enough so that parents may ask the church and church school to supplement what they are doing in the family. The job will be on the way to accomplishment when the church can ask the home, "What do you parents want us to do to supplement your work in Christian education?"

THE CHURCH

Responsibility for Christian education also rests, of course, with the church. There are certain tasks that the church shares; others that are distinctively its own. The church is responsible, along with other community groups, for the development of character and moral and spiritual qualities in life. The roots of moral character are laid in childhood and youth. Some shared and co-ordinated approach to the matter is only common sense.

Neither does the church have sole responsibility for the teaching of Christian truth, for the home shares in it. It is likely that even though Christian truth is learned in the church it may not be indelibly impressed upon the mind, heart, and spirit of the child if the home is not co-operating completely in the process.

But the church does have distinctive Christian education responsibilities. It is its responsibility to represent the Christian faith in the entire community, to stand as a symbol and to act as a force within the community for the Christian way and the Christian life.

The church has a responsibility that cannot be delegated for gathering up in the experience of group worship all those strands of experience which go to make up the individual's consciousness of God. We pray and worship in private; if we prayed and worshiped only in public, our spiritual life would be thin indeed. But we need the experience of great common worship, worship with others who seek together with us and who share our points of view, aims, and aspirations. We need the experience of bringing our ideals and aspirations corporately into the presence of God that there by his will and spirit they may be evaluated and redeemed.

Furthermore, we need the sense of a great company of believers and fellow Christians extending into the community, throughout the world, and into history. The church alone, in its nurture, can give us the sense of having things in common, a fellowship with others throughout the entire world, the sense of citizenship in a Kingdom that, while it is not of this world, nevertheless is a Kingdom expressing itself throughout the world as the Church of Jesus Christ.

Beyond the local church there are interchurch councils organized within the community, whose tasks include a number of concerns, whose responsibilities cover a number of needs that cannot be met by local churches alone. Evangelism cannot be carried on very successfully in many communities except by all the groups that are concerned working together. The task of leadership education is one that, while it may be done by the local church, is better done in many cases by the churches of the community working together through their interchurch council. When we come together in leadership schools and in community leadership meetings, we get the sense of oneness, the sense of mutual aim and support, that we so badly need.

The denominations have responsibility for determining general policy in Christian education and for providing curriculum, supervision, and various kinds of administrative direction for the program as it affects the local church. They also have a responsibility for transcending their own bounds in participating in those regional, national, and world councils where general direction, co-ordination, and supervision may be achieved.

THE COMMUNITY AND THE SCHOOLS

In the community the influence of the neighborhood on religious attitudes is important. The influence of the play group, friends on the playground or street, cannot be minimized. But the predominant influence in many of our neighborhoods at present is not Christian; it is secular. We have such heterogeneous neighborhoods that the practice and discussion of religion has become almost taboo among adults, though not among children. The general atmosphere is such that it does not add greatly to an appreciation of the Christian way of life or Christian truth. Its influence, however, may be as telling as any other except the home, and its responsibility comparably great.

The schools are responsible for certain contributions to religious nurture and Christian education. There are, of course, certain aspects of Christian education with which the schools may not deal. Our public schools are nonsectarian; they are not allied and cannot be allied with any particular faith. Therefore we cannot expect the school to do Christian education of the sort required of the church and home.

The schools are responsible, however, for teaching informationally about religion. While they teach about government, industry, and commerce, they often ignore churches. They might well teach comparative religion. How may international affairs be understood if the beliefs and motivations of the peoples of the world are not known? Practical steps to do this are being taken, though the difficulties are great.

Religious issues should be faced when they arise in the school curriculum. How may English literature be taught honestly without dealing with its religious implications? The same holds for science, history, music, and art — to mention only a few subjects.

The task of the schools includes moral and spiritual education. We cannot afford a characterless generation, or one indifferent to the values upon which our culture and civilization depend. The schools must teach to the point of those religious commitments which undergird all our common aspirations and social attainments.

The college or university level of experience is particularly significant for Christian education for maturity. It is often the only opportunity for clarifying religious thinking and integrating it with scientific, philosophical, and professional ideas. While the Church-related college has a clear responsibility for Christian education, both in instruction and in leadership education, the State and non-Church-related school must also make appropriate curricular and extracurricular provision to meet this need.

The community itself has responsibility for its moral tone and for the spiritual encouragement of its people. It may hardly be indifferent or hostile to organized religion. All its moral force should be used to back religious education in school, church, synagogue, and home.

Where, in the long run, does responsibility for Christian education rest? It rests upon the concerned individual. It is he who takes leadership responsibility for it in the home, church, interchurch council, neighborhood, school, community, denomination, and those councils that guide the Church nationally and internationally. The ultimate responsibility for Christian education is ours individually. It becomes mine as I become Christian, responding to God in loving and voluntary obedience. Those who have responded to the call of Christ recognize as an important part of their commitment the task of working through all these responsible agencies, that the aims of Christian education may be accomplished.

Chapter 17

EMERGING OPPORTUNITIES

A FORWARD LOOK in Christian education requires that the most significant and promising emerging opportunities for development be outlined and analyzed. This chapter, while it cannot pretend to include all the new opportunities for Christian education, attempts to select and discuss those that seem to be most important and that have not been dealt with elsewhere in the book.

AUGMENTING THE SUNDAY SCHOOL

The Sunday school is no longer enough. This is true, in part, because it has ceased to be the independent agency it once was, operating parallel to the church. It has become the Sunday church school, working to accomplish the educational aims of the church under the church's supervision and direction. But even the Sunday church school is not enough if by it we mean the hour or hour-and-a-half affair that meets on Sunday.

There are several reasons why the Sunday church school is not enough. It is not reaching the children, youth, and adults of the nation. The figures show that, while it is growing, there are vast numbers outside it. There is little attempt to help them to come to it, and it is not going to them.

The Sunday school never provided enough time to do the job of Christian education, and the Sunday church school has not done much better. The time allotted is not sufficient to accomplish the purposes involved.

Neither the Sunday school nor the Sunday church school has

been impressive enough to do the job. To our pupils, real life pulses in the community outside the school, and the church school is regarded as an artificial affair. Go into some of our public schools, see the kind of work being done there, the seriousness with which it is taken by the pupils, and the attractive surroundings in which it is done. Then come back to the cellars in which many of us still attempt to work and watch the amateurish fumbling with education that goes on in many of them. They become objects of shame to us. Can they be anything different to our pupils?

What directions are we taking in the matter of augmenting the Sunday church school? The most obvious is the so-called "expanded session," where the Sunday church school meets for two and a half to three hours on Sunday morning, and includes a variety of educational activities in its program. This plan has been widely adopted by Jewish groups, but has not been very popular with Protestants. Interference with teachers' attendance at the morning worship service and the inability of many volunteer teachers to use the added time profitably are among the reasons for its failure to gain wide acceptance.

The weekday church school is used: released-time and after-school education. In many cities and towns there is a competence and dignity about weekday religious education, and a community concern for it, that is lacking in the case of the Sunday church school. An exceptionally promising possibility is the combination of released-time and after-school education to give as much as a three-hour continuous period for Christian education one afternoon per week during the school year.

Religious education in the home is advocated, but for all our efforts we have hardly scratched the surface. The family is recognized as the basic unit in society, yet its disintegration during the past few decades is obvious. Church, community, and nation are concerned about it and have been seeking practical means for renewing creative family life. A few suggestions have been made that the average church family can use. But effective Christian education demands an approach that will not only use the home, but will make it central, the most important relationship in Christian education and the source of its vitality.

The vacation church school is remarkably successful. Occasionally it occurs to us that in those few days in the summer we offer more consistent, thorough, and realistic work than we do on Sundays during the entire year.

A limited number of parochial schools have been established. In general, Protestants feel that devotion to the democratic community means support of the public schools. But there are some groups, and a growing number of local churches, that are convinced that the task of Christian education requires that all schooling be permeated with distinctively Christian values, expressed as such.

The weekday church nursery school is a promising innovation. Where the public schools provide kindergartens for five-year-olds, the church nursery school is likely to be limited to three- and four-year-olds; otherwise the age range is three through five. Increased knowledge of the preschool child leads to the conclusion that these years are psychologically crucial for the development of religion. It is then that important emotional patterns are set, that the roots of faith expressed in nonverbal terms begin to grow, and that the individual is introduced to the demands and opportunities of the society and culture in which he is to live. That education during these years should be the concern of the church, and that the introduction to church Christian education should be a five-day-a-week affair under church sponsorship and direction, and with full home co-operation, is becoming an accepted principle.

In exploring the place of religion in the public schools the public school people themselves are taking the lead. Significant things have been done by the National Education Association, which published the guide entitled *Moral and Spiritual Values in the Public Schools* (Washington, D.C., 1951). The American Council on Education has conducted widespread research which has resulted in the publication of *The Relation of Religion to Public Education, The Basic Principles,* and *The Function of the Public Schools in Dealing with Religion* (Washington, D.C., 1949 and 1953). Grass-roots experimentation is being carried on in several states and many communities, using a variety of approaches and materials. (See William Clayton Bower, *Moral and Spiritual Values in Education*. University of Kentucky Press, 1952).

The reconstruction of a varied and complete church program for youth will become more important in the next few years. In the last few years our seemingly dwindling youth work has been a source of discouragement. But the youth population itself has been dwindling. It is apparent from the present population figures that it is time for vigorous reorganization of youth work in order to be ready to take care of the larger numbers coming on. A revitalized youth work may gain such momentum that it will reach a larger proportion of the youth of the land than at present. Gaining such momentum will depend upon the capability of the leaders, the realism of the program, and, above all, the centrality of thoroughgoing community evangelism.

Recently steps have been taken to renew adult Christian education. Some of the first efforts at adult education in this country were motivated by the need for adult Christian education. The summer assemblies at Chautauqua, and the dissemination of their cultural and religious benefits throughout the nation for decades, were carried forward out of a deep sense of the need for the Christian education of adults. For some years church adult work has been declining, while adult education in the community at large has been increasing. The recent moves toward reorganization have taken several forms: work with young adults and young married couples, organized work for men as well as women in the church, and group programs for older persons.

But if we are merely to augment the Sunday school, we shall fail to accomplish anything of lasting significance. If, on the other hand, our concern leads to a new idea of the Christianization of the whole life of every child, youth, and adult in the community, then we are on the way to greatly increased effectiveness. The result may well be almost complete reorganization, perhaps putting the home first, giving new emphasis to the community, and expanding the services of the church itself.

DEVELOPING A SOUND LEADERSHIP STRATEGY

No statistical increase in the number of persons reached will mean anything unless steps are taken to improve the quality of the program's leadership. This requires a sound strategy for the development of new leaders and constant improvement of the work of those already on the job.

The Jewish groups have almost completely abandoned volunteer leadership in principle and practice. They saw that it was not doing the job they wanted done. Determined to do the job seriously, they have taken steps to develop a professional leadership and to put their schools into trained hands.

The Roman Catholic Church similarly has little faith in the volunteer. Its teaching orders staff not only its vast system of parochial and boarding schools and colleges, but also its Sunday schools, where they are still deemed necessary as temporary expedients.

We Protestants put our faith in the volunteer teacher and leader. Do we have a defensible basis for doing so? Not unless certain conditions are met. The first condition would be met if Christian education activities were regarded as a part of the life of the church as a family, or as an extension of the fellowship of the family. If the family atmosphere is to be maintained in the church, not only is there a place for intelligent and trained volunteer leadership, but overprofessionalization will actually destroy it.

The second condition involves training. If volunteers can be effectively trained, there is a lasting place for them. But training means more than a few courses for lay people. It means thorough understanding of principles and methods, on-the-job training, and access to adequate supervision.

The principle of volunteer leadership is sound only under such conditions. Yet our churches are far from meeting even this common-sense standard. Many teachers are not aware of the prin-

ciples basic to their work. They are not systematically introduced
to a variety of methods, with guidance as to their appropriate
selection and use. They are not sent to laboratory or demonstra-
tion schools to watch successful teachers at work. Furthermore,
the vast group of our leaders have no access at all, to say nothing
of adequate access, to supervision.

Adequate access to supervision means at least a greatly enlarged
supervisory staff, local or regional; plenty of resources readily
available (books, magazines, pictures, stories, audio-visuals, project materials, experts); and frequent personal- and group-plan-
ning conferences and clinics.

In a community with several churches and no professional
Christian educator, supervision may well be on an interchurch
basis, through the full-time services of a competent director of
Christian education for the community.

In rural areas such services may be provided on a regional,
sectional, or neighborhood basis. The larger parish plan and the
co-operative parish plan provide for this kind of supervisory service and leadership training. The larger parish plan involves the
co-ordination of the programs of all the churches in a community
or section, in order to enrich the impact of the church upon the
community and enhance its services through the use of a diversi-
fied ministry. In the larger parish, one minister may be an administrator, another an educator, a third an evangelist and counselor.
A director of Christian education should be a member of the
staff. Often larger parishes are interdenominational. The co-operative parish plan involves the banding together of all the
churches in an area to plan, carry through, and staff their Christian education program together. Often the executive of the co-
operative parish is the professional director of Christian education.

If supervision cannot be done locally, then the denomination
should increase its supervisory services on a regional basis. Every
teacher and leader in every church should have access to as much
supervisory help as he needs, when and where he needs it. It
should be available, not remote; at hand, not in an office in some
distant city.

Adequate supervision also means plenty of resources, right at hand. The kind of curriculum we use calls for enriched pupil experience and for methods that require resources not previously used. Part of the supervisor's task is to have them ready for use when they are needed. He performs an invaluable service in knowing them accurately enough to be able to recommend appropriate resources for each need.

Frequent personal and group conferences and clinics are called for. Planning conferences (preview or coaching conferences) are for the purpose of planning specific lessons or units so that the teacher may be able to initiate and carry them through with good results. Clinics are for the purpose of reviewing work already done, thinking and working it over, in order to gain insight on what needs to be done to improve it. Of late we have become fairly skilled in the use of planning conferences, but we have not been very good at clinics. This correlates with a general decline in interest in evaluation, an interest that should be speedily revived.

Depending on volunteers is rather dangerous. We cannot afford it unless it be to build and maintain the family atmosphere in the educational program in our churches. We do not depend on them in any other important educational situation. In any case they must be trained and adequately supervised. Our insurance is to put at their disposal adequate materials, resources, and supervisory personnel. Anything less is to fail the church and to fail them.

Why emphasize these mechanics? Why stress organization? What is being urged is not the mechanics of Christian education, but its dynamics; not mere organization, but the building of a structure that will sustain new life.

EDUCATING AND EVANGELIZING THE INDIVIDUAL

The importance of individual experience has always been recognized in Protestant theory and practice, but the recognition now being given to individual education and evangelism has been markedly influenced by advances in psychology, by the practice of guidance, and by new interpretations of the evangelistic needs of modern children, youth, and adults.

What are some of the new trends in the education of individuals in the Christian life? The practice of guidance is rapidly being developed. It is being used in a few Christian education programs and should be used in many more. Guidance seeks to aid the individual in making needed adjustments to his society, in bringing information to him that will help him to make necessary decisions, and in assisting him toward the emotional security basic to creative living. It is problem-centered, but deals primarily with the problems of normal people in normal life situations. Christian educators would do well to master the tested techniques of individual and group guidance, in order to use them in the guidance of individuals under their care into the fullness of Christian living.

The practice of counseling is often a part of the guidance procedure, but is used extensively to help those whose problems are overpowering them, leading them into serious maladjustments and mental and emotional difficulties. It is most important for the Christian educator to know how much he may safely undertake in counseling, what methods to use, and how to know when to refer the individual to a fully trained and competent professional counselor. As a rule he may use both direct and indirect methods: direct, when specific instructions and help are called for and the individual has sincerely asked for them; indirect, when he and the individual are exploring the problem together to try to understand it and gain personal insight into the factors involved. He should be briefed on the symptoms of those difficulties which are beyond his ability to handle, and informed how such cases may be referred properly to those equipped to handle them.

Christian educators have not often thought of guidance and counseling as part of their task. It has taken years to convince the Church that the nurture of the Christian life requires the individual approach in many cases, and is facilitated by it in most cases. To lead boys and girls, men and women, to full life in Christ means more than seeing that they attend meetings and classes, and much more than mere persuasive personal contact at critical moments of decision.

An interesting development is the discovery of the effectiveness of work within a group in helping the individual to find himself and deal with his problems. Significant areas have been defined: group work, group guidance, and group dynamics. All these approaches are built upon the principle that personality change and development very often take place best in the give-and-take of persons of the same general level of development or experience, or among persons facing the same type of problem, if the individual can develop a feeling of trust and confidence in the group.

Group work is a method that has been used primarily with difficult children and youth, sometimes delinquents or predelinquents, to lead them within a group experience to find constructive channels for the release of their hostilities and aggressions. It usually starts with some activity in which all will participate eagerly (perhaps a sport, club, or other recreational activity) and builds into activities in which the skills of social responsibility are learned and the individual and the group are helped to see and practice their constructive roles in society. Group work should not be allowed, however, to come to mean exclusively work with difficult and delinquent groups. Neither should it be allowed to come to mean work with children and youth exclusively.

Groups are found to be helpful in supplementing the processes of individual guidance and counseling. Thus group guidance is coming into use. There comes a time in the counseling process when shared problems and ideas are seen in a new light. A group of persons who are seeking answers to the same sort of problem may be of help to each other in attaining creative new adjustments. Group sessions are often led by the counselor. There is real merit in using the method with groups seeking to deal with individual problems, whether or not there has been individual counseling.

Group dynamics is a technique being experimented with by

social scientists primarily interested in relieving group tensions. It is also useful to the general practice of Christian education, since it seeks to substitute democratic methods of problem-solving for the autocratic handling of difficulties. It assumes that everyone involved with a particular problem has a stake in its solution and a contribution to make to it. By setting up the conditions of friendliness, and following scrupulously the processes of group thinking and group decision, this technique seeks to lead to the kind of solutions that will be agreed to and heartily followed by all concerned.

It will take some experimenting with guidance, counseling, and group methods to discover exactly how they may best be used in Christian education, but approaches like these have long been sought by those interested in effective work with individuals. To help the individual to come to the experience of salvation is the aim of Christian nurture as it explores their further use.

What is the new approach to evangelism in Christian education? The traditional concern of Protestantism for the individual has been expressed in evangelistic endeavor. Protestant Christian education is unthinkable except in terms of evangelism. However, great strides have been made in implementing the evangelistic aim through education.

Educational evangelism seeks to reach every boy, girl and adult for Christ. It seeks to do so with a full understanding of the readiness of the individual for Christian experience. It does not try to use grown-up concepts or foster grown-up experience among children. Neither does it seek to feed the adult on spiritual food suited to babes. It is the planned program of leading the individual to recognize and acknowledge the reality and truth of Christ for himself in terms that will capture him in an all-embracing commitment, one that will grow as he grows but will always be a commitment to the full living of the life in Christ. This kind of evangelism is a part of the ongoing responsibility of the home, every facet of the church's educational program, and of the Church at large.

With the concern for educating and evangelizing the individual, the need for institutional effectiveness is re-emphasized. Where we have done an ineffective job with individuals it has been because we have not organized the institutional program definitely to serve individuals. A reconstitution of aim in terms of service to them will result in a functional reorientation of the program and the institutions that constitute and promote it.

RELIGION IN HIGHER EDUCATION

Religion is now being seriously reintroduced into the life and curriculum of American schools and colleges: state, private, and Church-related. There appear to be four prevailing views on the place of religion in higher education.

In some institutions, religion is not recognized as having a place in a supposedly scientifically oriented higher education.

In others, religion is taught about, scientifically and appreciatively, as an aspect of our present culture and as an important factor in understanding the past. Religious values are to be highlighted in the teaching of English, history, art, music, science, and the like. This is a promising approach and appeals widely to those who are just beginning to work with religion in college. It would appear to be a most suitable approach for the state-supported school.

In a third group, the religious values in the life of the school community (the student council, teams, extracurricular service projects, and other extracurricular activities) are to be developed consciously in order that the individual may through participation in them be helped to become a person of character. Sometimes the conscious and avowed aim is the development of Christian character. This and the second group are not mutually exclusive.

There is a fourth group in which Christian commitment is recognized as one of the necessary aims of the school, and the whole life of the school attempts to express and lead toward this commitment. There are a few schools that have come to this point, most of them being specifically Church-related institutions.

These institutions are free thus to experiment with the close integration of Christian faith and life and higher education, and have a responsibility for doing so.

There is a concern for the curricular implementation of the new interest in religion and higher education. The minimum essentials for courses in religion might well be the following. First, the standard sciences of religion: comparative religion, which considers the religions of the world for what they are and broadly surveys contemporary religious experiences; history of religion, which goes by way of depth into the development of religion from the beginning of recorded time; psychology of religion, which deals with the phenomena of individual religious behavior and development; and sociology of religion, which studies the phenomena of the social organization of religion and the relationships of religion and society. Secondly, philosophy of religion, which is the systematic treatment of the religious aspects of the problems of ultimate reality, knowledge, and value. Ordinarily in school and college this approach is more appropriate than the normative study of theology, although there is a trend toward courses definitely theological in character. Finally, the Bible, taught not just as literature, not as background for understanding literary allusions, nor even for the beauty of its lines, but as the source of the profound religious ideas that have motivated and directed men in Christ throughout the ages.

Around an essential structure such as this may be built a curriculum in religion for higher education that will provide those rich, challenging, and integrating experiences which must characterize a committed Christian leadership adequate to tomorrow's needs.

Part Five

CONCLUSION

Chapter 18

THE NURTURE OF THE CHRISTIAN LIFE

THE PURPOSE OF THIS BOOK has been to develop a theory for Christian education based upon an appraisal of its aims and present condition, an understanding of the nature of the life of Christ, an analysis of the ways in which personality is reconstructed and redeemed, and a consideration of several of Christian education's more important practical aspects. Each of these will now be summarized in order to give a brief statement of the theory involved.

THE STATUS OF CHRISTIAN EDUCATION

The modern Christian educator is now at a point where, after almost twenty years of discussion and debate, he is building on theoretical and practical foundations on which there is some degree of general agreement. The period of the flowering of religious education, which reached its climax in the 1920's, was followed by a period of curtailment and uncertainty. The tensions of the depression and the rediscovery of theology were to some extent released in the past decade by serious and thoroughgoing restudy.

The aim of Christian education is to nurture the Christian life. The purpose of all of education is that we may know the truth and become free through allegiance to it. Since, for Christians, God in Christ is the truth, the aim of Christian education is that we shall know the Christ and become free through whole and complete allegiance to him and his way. In broad terms, this involves Christian instruction, the redemption of the individual, and the redemption of society.

In practice Christian education should be carried on systematically and with careful planning. Objectives are set with both the Christian faith and the nature and needs of the pupil in mind. These objectives need to be translated into the planned experiences for Christian growth that constitute the curriculum, which in turn uses rich subject matter and a varied selection of appropriate methods. The process is to be organized (set up to accomplish its objectives), administered (effectively managed), supervised (kept up to standard democratically and co-operatively), and evaluated (subjected to periodic checks to see how well its results match its objectives).

THE CHRISTIAN LIFE

The life in Christ is the goal of Christian education. High value is to be placed on religion, which is devotion to the highest one knows or can conceive. But it is recognized that religion that is not Christian is not enough, since in Christ the meaning of life and history are revealed and God's redemptive love is made manifest.

There is no necessary separation between content and experience in Christian education. Christianity is a faith to be lived and taught. Minimizing either phase is likely to weaken the process. The Christian faith is rich in subject matter, and the Christian teacher is challenged to be a teacher of history, literature, the arts, philosophy, and theology.

The Bible is indispensable to the Christian life. Through it, the living Christ, and the Holy Spirit, God speaks his word to us. It provides the norm for the values to be developed in individual and social living, as well as the norm for the doctrines we are to teach. It gives the Christian a panoramic view of the redemptive purpose and action of God in history.

Christian education is best carried on as nurture within a fellowship. The fellowship of the Christian life is the Church — the cloud of witnesses around, the community of the faithful together with their children, the holy catholic Church, the Church of Jesus Christ, and the fellowship of love. It is the function of the Church to realize the will of God through the spirit of the living Christ in a dedicated society, to nurture the young in that dedicated society, and through it to represent its living Lord in the world.

Man's search for truth, beauty, and goodness is carried on with the aid of experience, reason, intuition, and revelation. But the Christian comes to know that his search is in reality but a response to God's search for him. The search is never finished, but in it firm beliefs are formed — beliefs that spell conviction, integrity, and effectiveness.

Naturalism, humanism, secularism, and totalitarianism have answers for life's fundamental questions. But the Christian answer is that I know myself, my society, my universe, and life's purpose when I live in Christ. The God of righteousness, truth, and love does not keep himself hidden. He reveals himself to us in Christ. The teacher, knowing Christ himself and seeking by his help to grow in full Christian living, helps the child to know what Christ did, helps the youth to know who Christ is and to live in him, and helps the grown person to increase ever in the spiritual life in him.

THE TRANSFORMATION OF PERSONALITY

Personality is the characteristic of free, responsible individuals as each responds uniquely to the opportunities and demands of nature, man, and God. What it may become is the restored image of God, taking on in each case the distinctive form that is fitting to the individual's experience.

The clue to personality is the developing self, which uses the " givens " of heredity and environment in terms of its goals and purposes. It makes use of many elements: biological dispositions; interaction with a specific environment; consciousness; unconscious dynamics; conflict, tension, and problems; integration; and membership character. Its essential function is the organization of experience through interpreting it, responding selectively to it, and systematizing it into meaningful and useful habits and concepts. Personality develops, with continuity from birth on, an essential unity and integrity that is basically individual.

Personality becomes Christian as experience is reconstructed, transformed, and redeemed by God in Christ. It develops through faith, belief, and growth in the Christian way of life; through the expression of Christian values and meanings through a variety of mediums; and through participation in the creation of a Christian society. This means that it comes into being as, through the Holy Spirit, God in Christ becomes the definitive reality in life to the child, youth, and adult.

The most meaningful education, then, is education for the life in Christ. Awareness of this central purpose guides the leader as he works. He pays close attention to individual growth in the life in Christ, and so orders the institutional aspects of the process that they may in themselves be effective expressions of his aims.

Specific Concerns

Among the more important specific problems of Christian education today are the planning of the curriculum; the development and selection of effective methods; the location of responsibility for the process in the individual himself, the home, the church, the community, and the schools; and certain emerging possibilities that present significant challenges.

Among these new opportunities are the following: The principle of the unity of experience within the personality implies that work must be done to augment the Sunday school and to co-ordinate the many developing aspects of the program under focal aims and procedures. Concentrated attention must be given to the problem of the improvement of leadership, conserving the values of volunteers but vastly increasing the professional resources available. Individual guidance and group methods need to be incorporated into the fabric of our work, not merely added to it. Finally, strategic importance lies in the curricular and extracurricular approaches of higher education to religion.

THE PRICE OF SUCCESS

No one can claim complete success in the practice of Christian education. The degree to which we are successful depends, however, upon our awareness of the conditions for success and our willingness to pay the price involved in meeting them.

We need clear and correct perspective on how Christian education takes place. The most influential force is not the teacher, superintendent, or parent, but God himself. We live in a world in which the most pervasive reality is the presence and power and will of God. The living Christ is a reality among us, he who can take hold of the child, the youth, and the adult, and make him his. If the parent, superintendent, or teacher is really serious about doing his job, then he is constantly trying to help the individual to become receptive to the reality of God. To lead and guide the pupil to the place where he may experience the reality of God, know something of his will, love him, and serve him directly: this is our task. We are guides and leaders; we are those who have the opportunity to lead others into an experience that is for them a direct opening of the resources that God in Christ has for them.

To meet the conditions for success, we can create in the home, church school, and other activities an atmosphere of receptivity; use the best curriculum and methods available; take advantage in our worship of all the resources of deep spirituality that are actually present or potential in the lives of the pupils as they gather together; observe the principles of utility, adequacy, and attractiveness so far as buildings, equipment, and other resources are concerned; and provide adequate financial support.

We can meet the conditions of training: preliminary training and continuous in-service training. The conditions of supervision, able, available, adequate, and democratic, can be met. We can know the individual and the group, plan the program in terms of their nature and needs, and meet the needs that arise for children, youth, and adults because of the kinds of communities in which they live.

Christian education must become a part of our basic commitment to Christ. Every Christian who has educational ability and who is wholly committed to Christ knows that that commitment carries with it educational responsibility. Perhaps responsibility may be taken for evangelism, for some aspect of the educational program, or in some other informal way. But the commitment is there: it is a commitment to lead and guide others into the Christian life.

This commitment to Christian education must be a central commitment of the Church itself. If certain other aspects of its program come and go, Christian education stays. It is one of the most central, significant, crucial functions that the Church has to perform.

SUGGESTED READINGS

SUGGESTED READINGS

THIS LIST of suggested readings represents a careful selection of what the author considers to be the best of the hundreds of volumes available. Many familiar volumes have been omitted because the problems or areas they deal with are better represented by a volume included on this list. Only one book representing a given topic, area, or need has been included.

Bowman, Clarice M., *Ways Youth Learn*. Harper & Brothers, 1952.
> The outstanding practical handbook on the Christian education of youth.

Coe, George Albert, *A Social Theory of Religious Education*. Charles Scribner's Sons, 1917.
> The religious education classic, still full of good, new ideas for the Christian educator.

Fallaw, Wesner, *The Modern Parent and the Teaching Church*. The Macmillan Company, 1946.
> The theory and practice of Christian family life and its relation to the church.

Gwynn, Price H., Jr., *Leadership Education in the Local Church*. The Westminster Press, 1952.
> A comprehensive guide to the training of teachers and other leaders.

Heim, Ralph D., *Leading a Sunday Church School*. The Muhlenberg Press, 1950.
> A solid treatment of every phase of church school work.

Lindhorst, Frank A., *The Minister Teaches Religion*. Abingdon Press, 1945.
> A little book that succeeds in pointing up what Christian education sets out to do and how its aims are accomplished.

Lotz, Philip Henry (ed.), *Orientation in Religious Education*. Abingdon Press, 1950.
> The " biggest " book on religious education now available. Forty-six authorities contribute articles touching a wide and well-chosen variety of topics.

Sherrill, Lewis Joseph, *The Struggle of the Soul*. The Macmillan Company, 1951.
> An outline of the Christian development of the individual through each stage of life.

Smart, James D., *The Teaching Ministry of the Church*. The Westminster Press, 1954.
> A crystallization of current thinking on theology and Christian education theory.

Vieth, Paul H. (ed.), *The Church and Christian Education*. The Bethany Press, 1947.
> The authoritative summary of the findings of the Study of Christian Education sponsored by the International Council of Religious Education.